What's Cooking?

What's Cooking?

FAVORITE RECIPES FROM AROUND THE WORLD

BY

Margaret Brink Warner

AND

Ruth Ann Hayward

Little, Brown and Company

BOSTON   LONDON   TORONTO

10 9 8 7 6 5 4

Library of Congress Cataloging in Publication Data

Main entry under title:

What's cooking?

    Includes index.
    Summary: A collection of recipes from more than thirty countries contributed by young people living in the United States who themselves, or whose parents, have emigrated to this country. Recipes vary from simple to complex and include information about their ethnic origins.
    1. Cookery, International—Juvenile literature. [1. Cookery, International]   I. Warner, Margaret Brink. II. Hayward, Ruth Ann.
TX725.A1W4   641.59   81–13709
ISBN 0–316–35252–7   AACR2

MV

Published simultaneously in Canada by Little, Brown & Company (Canada) Limited

PRINTED IN THE UNITED STATES OF AMERICA

To food lovers everywhere

Contents

Introduction

American teen-agers love to eat, but what is American food? Is it a hamburger? Is it ice cream? What about pizza, or pancakes? Actually, all those foods are as American as apple pie. Yet each of them, including apple pie, was brought here from another country. Apple pie came from Great Britain. Ice cream came from Spain. Pizza is Italian, and pancakes have their origin in French cooking.

No matter where you go in the United States, you can find food from other countries. Just as our language includes words from many other languages, American meals are a blend of foods from many countries. And this blend is what this cookbook is all about.

All the contributors to *What's Cooking?* are teen-agers who live in the United States. But either they or their parents or their grandparents came here from another country. We asked them to share their favorite family recipes so that you can sample the rich variety of foods immigrants brought with them. From Kugel Itriot (Israeli sweet noodle pudding) to Ogwono (African meat stew) to Gulnio Milanese (Italian fried chicken) you'll find lots of good cooking — and eating — for you, your family, and your friends. What's more, you'll meet some exciting young people from all over the United States through what they reveal about themselves, their families, and their recipes.

We hope this book will be an experience in good cooking and good eating, and a venture into serious cooking as well. The recipes included are authentic. Each represents years — sometimes generations — of experimentation with spices, sauces, and cooking times to satisfy a personal taste. Each recipe requires care and attention. But we guarantee that not one is beyond the skill of anyone who likes to eat.

Since the beginning of our history, nearly fifty million people have come to the United States to live, making this the largest melting pot — of people, of customs, and, of course, of food — the world has ever known. So . . . why not take the lid off the pot and see *What's Cooking?*

— *MBW and RAH*

What's Cooking?

Before You Get Started

You should find *What's Cooking?* easy to follow. It is designed to ensure success. The recipes are arranged by country of origin, and the countries are in alphabetical order. But if you should want, say, a hamburger or salad recipe, use the index in the back of the book.

Each recipe has two parts. "What You Need" tells what ingredients and what equipment you should have on hand before you start. "What You Do" explains step by step how to proceed.

In the section following this one (pages 7–9), you will find some helpful cooking hints. Cooking terms that might be unfamiliar are in the back of the book, along with a useful measurements table and party menu suggestions. And here are some general guidelines for you:

1. *Read the recipe carefully.* Read it through once, then again. Be sure you understand what is called for. Look up any unfamiliar terms in "Cooking Terms" (pages 153–156). From the preparation and cooking time given, figure out what time you need to start.

2. *Assemble the ingredients and equipment ahead of your starting time.* Check to see that you have everything you need. Be sure you have pots and pans of the right size. If you lack something and can't find a good substitute, ask an adult for advice.

3. *Follow the directions exactly.* Don't make any substitutions the first few times you cook. Each of the recipes has been carefully thought out — and they work. It's a good idea to prop the book open to the pages you are working from.

4. *Measure accurately.* The difference between a teaspoon and a tablespoon of sugar and salt in a recipe can mean the difference between a successful dish and a failure.

Make sure you have the proper measuring tools on hand. Measuring spoons should be used for any measurement, liquid or solid, of less than ¼ cup. Experienced cooks may be able to guess, say, when a recipe calls for ¼ teaspoon of pepper, but inexperienced cooks should measure accurately, not guess. To measure ¼ teaspoon of pepper, fill the ¼-teaspoon measuring spoon and run the edge of a knife or spatula across the spoon to level the pepper. If the recipe calls for, say, a heaping tablespoon of sugar, you do not, of course, level the sugar.

If you are measuring dry ingredients — flour, sugar, bread crumbs, rice — use graduated cups made of metal or plastic. These come in nests of ¼ cup, ⅓ cup, ½ cup, and 1 cup sizes. Fill the cup and level off the top with the edge of a knife or spatula. Or you may use a 1-cup measure that is marked in increments. In that case, set the cup on a flat surface and read the measure at eye level. Don't bang the cup to level the ingredient — it will settle, and you will end up adding too much.

Flour specifications can be tricky. If a recipe calls for 1 cup of sifted flour, you measure the flour *after* it has been sifted. But if it calls for 1 cup of flour, sifted, you sift the flour after you measure it. The distinction is an important one because sifted flour has more air in it and thus takes up more room than unsifted flour. One cup of unsifted flour contains more flour than does one cup of sifted flour.

Liquid ingredients — water, milk, oil — should be measured in a glass measuring cup marked in increments. Fill the cup to the measure you need, set the cup on a flat surface, and read the measure at eye level.

5. *Check the number of servings.* Use the number as a guide, not as a hard-and-fast rule. For example, if your friends, or family of four, are fond of second helpings (or heap the plate the first time around), you may want to increase the amount of *each* ingredient in the recipe.

The rest of the menu may make a difference, too. If you are planning to serve soup, salad, a main dish with a couple of vegetables, and a dessert, each portion need not be as large as if the main dish were the whole meal. In that case you may want to cut the recipe a bit. (Although leftovers can make great meals themselves.)

If you want to cut down or increase the size of a recipe, the table of equivalent measures on page 157 will be a great help. In general, to double a recipe, double each ingredient. To cut a recipe in half, divide each ingredient amount by two. You might want to write the new amounts in the book beside the original ones. That way you won't forget when you cook the recipe the next time.

Earlier we mentioned that you should follow each recipe exactly. And that's important. But once you've tried a dish a few times, you may want to make some subtle changes. After all, everyone's taste is different. You may like hot peppers. Someone else may hate garlic. So, if you want to experiment a bit, go right ahead. Imagination and experimentation — that's what make a good cook a great cook. And how important are cooks? Well, the English poet Edward Bulwer-Lytton had this to say a hundred years ago. We can't think of a better answer:

> *We may live without poetry, music and art;*
> *We may live without conscience and live*
> *without heart;*
> *We may live without friends; we may live*
> *without books;*
> *But civilized we cannot live without cooks.*

Helpful Hints

Deep-Fat Frying

Frying in deep fat is extremely dangerous. Do not attempt any recipes calling for it unless you have the proper equipment, as specified here, and your parents have given you permission to go ahead. Dress appropriately — do not wear clothing with loose sleeves — and tie long hair back. Before you start, read carefully the directions that follow.

In deep-fat frying there must be enough fat or oil to float the foods without crowding them. The temperature must be high enough to cook the foods quickly.

Cut foods into pieces about the same size. Pat them dry with paper towels (any water left on the food will cause the hot oil to spatter — and burn you). If you are deep-frying food that has been coated — with flour, bread crumbs, or batter — let it stand a few minutes so that the coating can set.

Use an electric deep-fat fryer with a temperature control. Read the manufacturer's directions with great care and follow them to the letter.

To prevent smoking, remove any loose food particles from the fat before adding the next batch of food.

Drain the fried food on paper towels.

If you wish to keep the food that has already been fried warm, place it on a baking pan in a 300° oven.

Used fat can be saved for another use by letting it cool, straining it through a strainer lined with a tissue or cheesecloth, and storing it, covered, in the refrigerator.

Separating Eggs

To separate an egg means to separate the yolk, or yellow part, from the white part. First set out two bowls, one for the yolk and one for the white. Then crack the egg in the middle by giving it a quick tap on the rim of one of the bowls. Using both hands, pull the shell apart gently, keeping the yolk in one of the halves. With a juggling motion, move the yolk to the other half-shell and back again, letting the white dribble down into its bowl. Keep passing the yolk back and forth until all the egg white has dripped into the bowl. If you get a little yolk in the white, scoop it out carefully with a corner of paper towel or a piece of egg shell.

Preparing Vegetables

All vegetables, with the exception of fresh mushrooms, should be washed before using to rinse off impurities. Root vegetables, such as potatoes and turnips, should be scrubbed with a stiff brush. Some vegetables should also be peeled, such as carrots, cucumbers, eggplant, garlic, onions, and sometimes potatoes. Certain ones need special treatment:

Broccoli and *cauliflower:* place them in a pot of salted water for 10-15 minutes to drive out any insects that may be in the heads.

Spinach: put it in a colander or sieve and run cold water over it to remove particles of sand.

String beans or *yellow beans:* snap the stem ends off and peel off the tough string on the side of the bean with a paring knife.

Mushrooms: clean them with a damp paper towel and cut off the tough end of the stem.

Skinning Tomatoes

Although raw tomatoes are eaten with the skin, some recipes in which tomatoes are cooked require that they be skinned. The skin can be removed easily if you blanch the tomato first. Boil enough water in a pot to cover the whole tomato. Pierce the stem end with a fork and plunge the tomato into the boiling water for 3-4 seconds. Then immediately run the coldest tap water over the tomato. Slip the skin off with a paring knife.

Whipping Cream

Use heavy cream or whipping cream for recipes calling for whipped cream. It is important that all utensils — mixing bowl and wire whisk (or egg beater or mixer blades) — be chilled in the refrigerator for 20-30 minutes before using them. A straight-sided bowl works best.

How much to whip? For topping on individual servings or pudding or fruit soup, whip ½ cup for 4 servings, ¾ cup for 6 servings, and 1 cup for 8 servings. For covering a 9-inch pie, whip 2 cups.

Pour the cream into the chilled bowl and whip it until it forms peaks.

To sweeten whipped cream, add sugar while you are doing the whipping. Add 1 teaspoon of sugar at a time, tasting after each addition to determine the desired amount.

Albania

Albania, where my mother and father were born and brought up, is a small country on the Adriatic Sea that is bordered by Greece and Yugoslavia. It is only a little bigger than Vermont and has only a few more people than Philadelphia.

I was born in New York City and lived in Brooklyn for a while. Then we moved to Dansville, New York, where we've been ever since. We own a motel — we live in part of it — and a restaurant. That is where I learned to cook.

Albanian food is simple but filling. Like their neighbors, the Greeks and the Yugoslavs, Albanians eat lots of onions, garlic, hot peppers, and lamb. Here are two favorite Albanian dishes I like to cook.

Bashkim Derti, 13

Chicken Soup
Corba

Preparation and cooking time: 3 hours   *Serves 4–6*

What You Need

2¼- to 3-pound stewing chicken or broiler-fryer
2 quarts of cold water
2 cups of white rice (not instant)
3 eggs
juice of 2 lemons, or 6 tablespoons of bottled lemon juice
salt and pepper

large pot with lid
measuring cup
large kitchen fork
large mixing spoon
large plate or shallow pan
small mixing bowl
lemon squeezer
wire whisk or fork
kitchen knife
cutting board

What You Do

1. Remove the giblets from the inside of the chicken and save for another use. Put the whole chicken in the pot with the water. Cover, and bring the water to a boil over high heat. Turn down the heat to low and simmer for 1½ hours.
2. Remove the chicken from the broth with the large fork and spoon and put it on the plate or in the pan to cool.
3. Add the rice to the broth and simmer, covered, for 1 more hour.
4. Break the eggs into the small bowl. Add the lemon juice and beat the mixture thoroughly with the wire whisk or fork. Then pour it into the rice and chicken broth and stir the mixture with the mixing spoon until it is well blended.
5. Remove the skin from the chicken and discard. Take the meat off the bones, cut it into bite-size pieces, and add them to the pot. Season with salt and pepper to taste, and stir thoroughly again.
6. If the soup has cooled, heat it to the boiling point. Serve it with hard-crust bread.

Stuffed Green Peppers
Dollma me Vaj

Preparation and cooking time: about 1½ hours   *Serves 6*

What You Need

½ cup of olive oil
1 cup of white rice (not instant)
1 large onion, chopped
2 cups of skinned, chopped tomatoes, canned or fresh (if fresh, see p. 8 for skinning instructions)
3 tablespoons of chopped parsley
2 tablespoons of lemon juice
½ cup of water
2 teaspoons of salt
6 medium-sized green peppers
hot water

kitchen knife
cutting board
large frying pan
measuring cup
long mixing spoon
measuring spoons
small spoon
large saucepan with lid

What You Do

1. Heat the oil in the frying pan over medium heat, add the onion, and cook it until soft. Add the rice and cook it until lightly browned.
2. Stir in the tomatoes, parsley, lemon juice, ½ cup of water, and salt. Bring to a boil. Cover the pan, reduce the heat to low, and let the mixture cook while you fix the peppers.
3. Rinse the peppers, cut the tops off and save them. Scoop out the seeds and the membranes and throw them away.
4. Using the small spoon, stuff the peppers loosely with the rice mixture. Replace the tops and stand the peppers side by side in the saucepan. Carefully pour hot water around the peppers until it reaches almost to the tops.

5. Cover the pan and cook over low heat for 30 minutes. Then sample the rice from one of the peppers. If the rice is tender and the mixture is fluffy, fine. If not, add a little more water to the pan, and continue cooking for a few more minutes.

Argentina

When I first arrived in the United States, I found that most people thought of Argentina as a country filled with adobe huts that had no electricity or running water. Quite the contrary, Argentina is a beautiful, modern country. Buenos Aires, the city where I lived, is a huge, metropolitan city quite similar to New York. You can even get Gucci shoes there!

The Argentine eating habits differ somewhat from those in America. We hardly ever ate breakfast in Argentina, and if we did, it usually was only a roll and coffee. I'll never forget my first encounter with Cheerios. I had never seen breakfast cereal before, and I loved it! I ate it nonstop for days.

The Argentine lunches don't differ very much from those in the United States, but we always had tea about five o'clock. We used to eat our dinner much later, about nine o'clock. Argentina produces a lot of cattle, so dinners consisted mostly of beef. We also used to have big barbecues quite often — not the standard barbecue, mind you — we ate the whole cow!

Although I'm not a great cook, I do love to eat all kinds of food. Here are two of my favorite Argentine recipes.

Silvia Lopez, 18

Fried Beef
Milanesas

> ### CAUTION!
> THIS RECIPE CALLS FOR FRYING IN DEEP FAT.
> DO NOT GO AHEAD UNTIL YOU READ PAGE 7.

Preparation and cooking time: about 1 hour   *Serves 6*

What You Need

1½ pounds of lean top round, cut into 6 thin pieces
salt and pepper
3 eggs
fine dry bread crumbs
oil

meat hammer or rolling pin
cutting board
small mixing bowl
wire whisk or fork
plate
electric deep-fat fryer
long-handled tongs
paper towels

What You Do

1. Pound each piece of beef on the cutting board with the meat hammer or the rolling pin until it is very thin, being careful not to tear the meat. Sprinkle each piece with salt and pepper.
2. Break the eggs into the bowl and beat them with the wire whisk or fork until they are well mixed. Spread the bread crumbs on the plate.
3. Dip each piece of beef first into the egg, then into the bread crumbs. Press the crumbs into the beef with your hand, making sure that each piece is thoroughly coated.
4. Pour 2 inches of oil into the fryer and heat according to the manufacturer's directions. When the right temperature is reached, *slowly* lower a piece of beef into the fat and fry until nicely browned, about 5 minutes in all. Turn once with the tongs to brown on both sides. Transfer the fried pieces to paper towels to drain.
5. Serve the beef with mashed potatoes and salad.

Meat Turnovers
Empañadas

Preparation and cooking time: about 1 ¾ hours

*Makes 20
turnovers*

What You Need

FOR THE PASTRY
2¼ cups of all-purpose
  flour
1 egg, beaten
½ cup of butter or mar-
  garine
1 teaspoon of salt
ice water

FOR THE FILLING
1 tablespoon of oil
1 medium-sized onion,
  finely chopped
2 cloves of garlic, finely
  chopped
1 pound of ground beef
1 teaspoon of salt
⅛ teaspoon of pepper
8 pitted black olives, quartered
3 hard-boiled eggs, finely
  chopped
flour

large mixing bowl
measuring cup
measuring spoons
waxed paper
large frying pan
long mixing spoon
rolling pin
cutting board
cup or jar 4 inches in
  diameter
small fork
baking sheet

What You Do

1. Make the pastry. In the bowl, mix the flour, egg, butter, and salt with your fingers. Add as little ice water as possible (about 2 tablespoons) to make a firm dough. Wrap the dough in waxed paper and chill it for 1 hour in the refrigerator.
2. Make the filling. Heat the oil in the frying pan and cook the onion and garlic over medium heat until the onion is soft.
3. Add the beef, salt, and pepper, and cook the mixture —

stirring constantly — until the ground meat is completely browned. Remove from the heat and mix in the olives and hard-boiled eggs. Set the filling aside.

4. Preheat the oven to 375°.
5. Lightly flour the rolling pin and cutting board. Roll out the dough on the board until it is ⅛ of an inch thick. Cut out circles with the cup or jar. Gather the scraps of dough into a ball, roll the ball out, and cut more circles.
6. Put 1 tablespoon of the filling in the center of each circle and fold the dough in half to make a turnover. Press the edges with the tines of the fork so they stay together.
7. Bake the turnovers on the baking sheet for about 12 minutes, until they are nicely browned. Serve them hot.

Australia

I left my home in Sydney, Australia, a year ago to work for the Australian Consulate in Washington, D.C. (With my last name, Washington seemed like the perfect city to come to!) I came by ship, which took about three weeks because we stopped in New Zealand, Fiji, and Vancouver, Canada. From Vancouver I took the Canadian railroad across the Rockies. It was mid-January, and was I ever in for a surprise when I felt the freezing temperatures and saw snow for the first time! Sydney is subtropical, and when I left just after Christmas, the temperature was in the high nineties.

After arriving in Washington, I met another Australian girl, and we rented an apartment with two girls from New Zealand. We take turns cleaning, shopping, and cooking.

When it's my turn to cook, I often make Batter-fried Fish and Potato Scallops, an Australian dish my mother taught me. Australians are also big meat eaters, and Carpetbag Steak is a traditional Australian recipe. Since the steak is stuffed with oysters, it recalls the carpetbags of the old-time peddlers, which were stuffed with samples of things to be sold.

Judy Washington, 18

Batter-fried Fish and Potato Scallops

CAUTION!
THIS RECIPE CALLS FOR FRYING IN DEEP FAT.
DO NOT GO AHEAD UNTIL YOU READ PAGE 7.

Preparation and cooking time: about 1 ¾ hours　　　　　*Serves 3–4*

What You Need

1 cup of flour

1 cup of milk

1 egg

pinch of salt

2–3 medium-sized potatoes

1 pound of fish fillets, such as cod, flounder, or haddock

1½ cups of oil

measuring cup

medium-sized mixing bowl

egg beater or wire whisk

vegetable brush

paper towels

kitchen knife

cutting board

electric deep-fat fryer

shallow baking pan

What You Do

1. Put the flour, milk, egg, and salt in the bowl. Beat the mixture with the egg beater or the wire whisk until smooth and let it stand for about 1 hour.
2. Preheat the oven to 300°.
3. Scrub the potatoes under running water, pat them dry with paper towels, peel them, and slice them thickly.
4. Pour the oil into the fryer and heat it according to the manufacturer's directions.
5. Dip the potato slices into the batter and then fry them until they are nicely browned. Don't forget to lower the basket *slowly* into the oil. When the potatoes are done, drain them on paper towels. Sprinkle them with salt, transfer them to the baking pan, and keep them warm in the oven while you fry the fish.
6. Check the manufacturer's instructions for the correct tempera-

ture for frying the fish and proceed accordingly. Pat the fillets dry with paper towels and carefully dip them into the batter. Fry them until they are nicely browned. Drain them on paper towels and serve them hot with the potatoes.

Carpetbag Steak

What You Need

2 pounds of rump steak, 1½ inches thick

8 oysters, shucked (about ½ pint), fresh, frozen, or canned

salt and pepper

2 tablespoons of butter

1 teaspoon of lemon juice

1 tablespoon of sherry

1 teaspoon of chopped parsley

kitchen knife

skewers or a large needle and strong thread

broiler pan, or rack and baking pan

measuring spoons

small saucepan

basting brush

kitchen fork

long mixing spoon

What You Do

1. With a sharp knife, make a slit in the side of the steak, halfway across, to form a pocket.
2. Season the outside of the steak and the pocket with salt and pepper.
3. Insert the oysters in the pocket. Skewer the edges together or sew them with the needle and thread. Melt the butter in the saucepan.
4. Put the steak on the broiler pan or on the rack in the baking pan, brush with the melted butter, and place under the broiler. Broil the steak, turning once with the fork, until it is done to your taste (5–8 minutes for rare; 8–12 minutes for medium; 12–15 minutes for well done). Remove the skewers or thread.
5. Add the lemon juice, sherry, and parsley to the juices left in the pan, mix well, and pour over the steak.
6. Serve with a tossed green salad and crusty bread.

Austria

According to my birth certificate, I am Austrian, but when I was born, my Austrian parents were living in Ankara, Turkey. I made my first friends there. They all came from different countries. Our neighbors on either side were Americans, and the people across the street came from Germany. Many of my friends were Turkish, and when I was five, I spoke the native language very well. Of course, I also used my mother tongue.

Later, we moved back to Austria, where I attended grammar school. I enjoyed having my grandparents live close by. My grandmother, a Viennese, prepares excellent dishes, and I learned to love this kind of cooking. When we came to the United States, we brought with us, among other things, many old Austrian recipes. Three of these I pass on to you. Try them. I think you will enjoy Austrian food as much as I do.

Felix Fischer, 16

Meat and Sauerkraut
Krautfleisch

Preparation and cooking time: about 1¾ hours   *Serves 3–4*

What You Need

½ pound of fat bacon
1 pound of lean pork
1 large yellow onion
1 small garlic clove
½ teaspoon of vinegar
½ teaspoon of salt
½ teaspoon of white pepper
½ teaspoon of caraway seeds
1 bay leaf
1 16-ounce can of sauerkraut
water

kitchen knife
cutting board
large frying pan with lid
measuring spoons
long mixing spoon

What You Do

1. Cut the bacon and pork into 1-inch cubes. Mince the onion and garlic.
2. Cook the bacon cubes over medium heat in the frying pan until they begin to shrink. Add the onion and brown slightly.
3. Stir in the garlic, vinegar, spices, herbs, and pork. Cover the pan and simmer the ingredients for about 30 minutes.
4. Stir in the sauerkraut, including the liquid from the can; then add enough water to cover the mixture. Simmer for 30 to 45 minutes, until most of the liquid has been absorbed and the pork is cooked through.

Ham Rolls
Schinkenröllchen

Preparation time: ¾ hour plus 2 hours or more for chilling the rolls

Serves 6–8

What You Need

12 very thin slices of Westphalian or baked ham
   (ask the butcher to do
   the slicing)
6 ounces of cream cheese,
   at room temperature
1 teaspoon of caraway
   seeds
3 tablespoons of sour
   cream
½ teaspoon of garlic pow-
   der
1 tablespoon of minced
   scallions
salt and pepper
1 bunch of watercress
   sprigs, trimmed to 2-
   inch lengths
pimento, green olives, or
   pickled mushrooms for
   decoration

kitchen·knife
cutting board
measuring spoons
small mixing bowl
long mixing spoon
toothpicks

What You Do

1. Trim the fat from the ham and cut the slices into strips 1½ inches wide. Try to keep the strips uniform in size.
2. In the bowl, mix the cream cheese with the caraway seeds, sour cream, garlic powder, and scallions. Season with salt and pepper to taste. If you are using Westphalian ham, be careful of the salt — the ham is very salty.
3. Spread 1 teaspoon of the cheese mixture all along one edge of a ham strip. Place a sprig or two of watercress on top of the cheese and roll up the ham, letting the watercress stick out at one end.

4. Decorate each roll with a piece of pimento, green olive, or pickled mushroom secured with a toothpick. Refrigerate the rolls for at least 2 hours before serving them as an hors d'oeuvre.

Viennese Veal Cutlets
Wienerschnitzel

Preparation and cooking time: about 1 hour (the veal must be refrigerated one more hour)   *Serves 4*

What You Need

2 pounds thin veal·cutlets
  flattened by the butcher
  to ⅛-inch thickness or
  less
1 egg
pinch of salt
flour
dry white bread crumbs
½ stick of butter or mar-
  garine
lemon slices

wire whisk or fork
medium-sized mixing bowl
2 plates
kitchen knife
cutting board
wire rack
serving plate
large frying pan
kitchen tongs

What You Do

1. Using the wire whisk or fork, beat the egg and salt together in the bowl. Spread some flour on one plate, bread crumbs on another.
2. Cut the veal into 8 or 12 even-sized pieces. One by one, dip the pieces in the flour (shake off the surplus), then in the beaten egg, and finally in the bread crumbs. Put the pieces on the wire rack and refrigerate them for 1 hour.
3. Put the serving plate in a 300° oven.
4. In the frying pan, heat the butter over medium-high heat until it sizzles. Quickly sauté the veal until golden brown, turning once with the tongs. Place the cooked pieces on the serving plate in the oven to keep warm while others are being fried.
5. Arrange the slices on the serving plate and garnish with lemon slices. The veal is good served with mashed potatoes and applesauce.

Canada

My grandmother was born in a little town near Toronto, Canada. As a young girl, she helped her mother prepare the meals served in her father's Red Lion Inn. Later her family moved to a farm in the fruit-and-vegetable–growing area along the shores of Lake Erie in New York State. When I was a little girl, I used to visit my grandmother in the summer. I remember her patience and encouragement when I wanted to help her cook.

Although I still love to cook and bake, much of my time during the school year is spent playing sports — soccer, volleyball, basketball, and softball. My five brothers and my mom are my best rooters.

Needless to say, we've all had to share the cooking and other household chores required by a large family. We have to "cook big" in our house and often use the same recipes Grandma did for feeding travelers and farmhands.

The Bread Pudding is a family favorite. It can be prepared ahead of time if you're rushed on the day you plan to serve it. My brothers say it tastes even better when it's a day old. The Vegetable Salad is a mainstay in any produce-growing area, but it can be made with canned or frozen vegetables if fresh ones are hard to find. The dressing makes this salad really special.

Susan Cowley, 17

Vegetable Salad

Preparation time: for raw salad, ¾ hour; for cooked, 1 hour (plus an additional hour for marinating)

What You Need

Use a combination of any of the following vegetables, preferably fresh, cut into bite-sized pieces. Allow ½ to 1 cup per person if the salad is a side dish, more for vegetable lovers. (See p. 8 for help in preparing the vegetables.)

asparagus
beans (green, yellow, lima)
beets
broccoli
carrots
cauliflower
corn
cucumbers
mushrooms
onions
peas
radishes
spinach
summer squash
tomatoes
zucchini

kitchen knife
cutting board
large saucepan with lid
large mixing bowl
medium-sized mixing bowl
measuring cup
measuring spoons
long mixing spoon
plastic wrap

DRESSING

1 cup of mayonnaise
1 tablespoon of cider vinegar
2 tablespoons of honey or brown sugar
2 teaspoons of prepared mustard
½ teaspoon of garlic powder
¼ cup of milk

What You Do

1. Wash and prepare the vegetables.
2. The vegetables can be used either raw or cooked. If you wish to

cook them, place them in the saucepan and add just enough water to cover them. Cover the pan and bring the water to a boil. Turn off the heat and let the vegetables steam for 10 to 15 minutes, depending on how crunchy you like them.

3. Drain the vegetables very well and place them in the large bowl.

4. Thoroughly mix the ingredients for the dressing in the smaller bowl.

5. Pour the dressing over the vegetables (use ¼ cup of dressing for every 2 cups of vegetables), cover the bowl with plastic wrap, and let the salad sit in the refrigerator for about 1 hour before serving it. If you wish, top the salad with croutons or nuts or both.

6. Store any leftover salad dressing in the refrigerator.

Bread Pudding

Preparation and baking time: 1½ hours   *Serves 8*

What You Need

3 cups of dry bread, cut into
   ½-inch cubes
1 quart of milk
1 tablespoon of melted butter or margarine
¼ teaspoon of salt
¾ cup of sugar or 1 cup of
   honey
3 eggs
1 teaspoon of vanilla
2 apples, diced
1 cup of raisins
1 teaspoon of cinnamon
1 teaspoon of nutmeg
cream or whipped cream
   (see "Whipping Cream,"
   p. 8)

kitchen knife
cutting board
measuring cup
1½-quart casserole
medium-sized saucepan
small mixing bowl
wire whisk or fork
measuring spoons
long mixing spoon
shallow baking pan

What You Do

1. Preheat the oven to 350°.
2. Grease the casserole with some extra butter or margarine and put in the bread cubes.
3. Pour the milk into the saucepan and heat it over medium heat until tiny bubbles appear around the edge.
4. Pour the milk over the bread cubes and let them soak for 5 minutes.
5. With the wire whisk, beat the eggs slightly in the small bowl.
6. Add the melted butter, salt, sugar (or honey), beaten eggs, vanilla, apples, raisins, and spices, and mix well.
7. Place the casserole in the baking pan, add hot water to a depth of 1 inch, and bake the pudding for 50 minutes, or until it is firm. Serve the pudding warm with cream or whipped cream.

China

Dad was born in Canton, China. Mom was born in New York, but she was raised in China. They came to the United States with my two sisters and brother. I am the first child in my family to be born here.

Food is very important to our family, and we are known for our incredible appetites.

Chinese cuisine has a wide range and variety. Each region of China has its own style of cooking. There are Cantonese, Szechuan, Hunan, and Mandarin, to name a few. Some of the cooking is spicy-hot. Some of it is mild. There is a saying, "If it can crawl, walk, slither, or swim, the Chinese can cook it." I personally don't practice that saying, but it's true.

Much equipment can be involved in Chinese cooking. There are the wok, the firepot, the bamboo steamer, and the vegetable cleaver. It's great if you have the equipment, but it's not really necessary.

The Chinese eat a lot of vegetables, but many of the vegetables, like bok choy, bamboo shoots, and snow peas, can be hard to find. The recipes I am suggesting are easy to make. The ingredients are easy to get. And the food is delicious!

Dayna Lee, 15

Chicken Wings
Chow Gai Yet

CAUTION!
THIS RECIPE CALLS FOR FRYING IN DEEP FAT.
DO NOT GO AHEAD UNTIL YOU READ PAGE 7.

Preparation and cooking time: ¾ hour   *Serves 4–6*

What You Need

12 chicken wings
1 cup of chopped onion
1 tablespoon of minced
  garlic
2 tablespoons of soy sauce
1 tablespoon of dry sherry
1 teaspoon of salt
1 tablespoon of sugar
1 teaspoon of sesame oil
1 teaspoon of pepper
1 teaspoon of powdered
  ginger
cooking oil

kitchen knife
cutting board
paper towels
measuring cup
measuring spoons
medium-sized mixing bowl
shallow baking pan
plastic wrap
electric deep-fat fryer

What You Do

1. Rinse the chicken. Pat it dry with paper towels.
2. Mix all the ingredients except the cooking oil in the mixing bowl. Dip the chicken in the mixture to coat each piece.
3. Place the chicken in one layer in the baking pan, cover with plastic wrap, and refrigerate overnight. It can be left for as long as three days — the longer, the better!
4. In the fryer, heat enough cooking oil to cover the chicken. Follow the manufacturer's directions for the correct temperature. Lower the basket *slowly* into the oil, and fry the chicken wings until they are very crispy and lightly browned.
5. Drain them on paper towels. Serve them hot as an appetizer or snack.

Shrimp with Ketchup
Ketchup Hung Su Har

Preparation and cooking time: ½ hour   *Serves 3–4*

What You Need

1 pound of shrimp, shelled
and deveined
1 teaspoon of soy sauce
⅓ cup of salad oil
2 cloves of garlic
3 thin slices of fresh ginger, or ½ teaspoon of
powdered ginger
1 medium-sized onion,
sliced into 6 pie-shaped
wedges
1 cup of ketchup

kitchen knife
cutting board
measuring spoons
measuring cup
large frying pan or wok
spatula

What You Do

1. In the frying pan, combine the soy sauce, oil, garlic, and ginger.
2. Add the onions. Bring the mixture to a boil over high heat, stirring constantly. The temperature should remain extremely hot through all steps.
3. Add the shrimp and stir-fry for 5 minutes.
4. Add the ketchup and continue stir-frying for 5 minutes more. Serve immediately as a main course with rice.

Beef and Broccoli

Preparation and cooking time: 1 hour   *Serves 3–4*

What You Need

½ pound of flank steak,
  sliced across the grain
  into slices ¼-inch thick
  (ask the butcher to do
  this)
2 tablespoons of cornstarch
2 teaspoons of soy sauce
5 tablespoons of salad oil
3 thin slices of fresh ginger
  (or 1 teaspoon of pow-
  dered ginger)
2 cloves of garlic
1 head of broccoli, cut into
  bite-sized pieces
½ cup plus 2 tablespoons of
  water

kitchen knife
cutting board
measuring spoons
medium-sized mixing bowl
large frying pan with lid
spatula
measuring cup

What You Do

1. In the mixing bowl, combine ½ tablespoon of cornstarch, 1 teaspoon of soy sauce, and 1 tablespoon of oil. Add the beef and soak for 15 minutes.
2. In the frying pan, heat over high heat 2 tablespoons of oil, the ginger, and the garlic until the mixture is sizzling.
3. Add the beef slices and stir-fry until the beef is barely pink. Remove the slices from the pan with the spatula and put them back in the bowl.
4. Heat the 2 remaining tablespoons of oil in the same pan. When sizzling, add the broccoli and stir-fry for 2 minutes. Add ½ cup of water, cover the pan, turn the heat to low, and let the broccoli steam for 3–4 minutes.
5. Add the rest of the soy sauce and a mixture of 1½ tablespoons of cornstarch and 2 tablespoons of water. Re-add the beef to the frying pan and stir-fry until the mixture thickens. Serve as a main course with rice.

CHINA ⟩ 35

Cuba

My family comes from Havana, the capital of Cuba, an island in the Caribbean off the coast of Florida. Although I was only six years old at the time, I can still remember leaving Havana with my family to come to the United States. Like many Cubans, we settled in Miami, Florida. Because so many Cuban people live there, a part of Miami is called Little Havana. But last year we moved to Connecticut, where I'm a sophomore at Danbury High School.

I like sports, especially tennis and football, girls, and cars. I'm saving my money so that I can afford to buy my own car when I'm old enough to drive. I have my own paper route, and I hope to get a part-time job after school when I'm sixteen.

Both my mother and my grandmother, who lives with us, are great cooks. I like to eat, and I especially enjoy Cuban dishes, which are very spicy. One of my favorite dishes is Pork, Cuban Style. When you make it, be sure to include the whole head of garlic, since that's what makes the recipe special. Black Beans and Avocado Salad complete the meal. If you were in Cuba, the dinner would be topped off with Cuban coffee, which is very strong and served in small cups. Most Americans find that it takes some getting used to.

Elio Manuel Capote, 15

Pork, Cuban Style

Preparation and baking time: 4½ hours (the pork must be   *Serves 8*
refrigerated for an additional 24 hours)

What You Need

1 6-pound leg of pork
1 head of garlic, peeled and
   finely chopped
1 teaspoon of salt
½ teaspoon of pepper
1 teaspoon of oregano
½ cup of lemon juice
3 large slices of onion

kitchen knife
cutting board
lemon squeezer
measuring spoons
measuring cup
small mixing bowl
long mixing spoon
shallow roasting pan
plastic wrap

What You Do

1. Make several shallow cuts in the meat with a sharp knife.
2. In the bowl mix the chopped garlic, salt, pepper, oregano, and
   lemon juice. Rub the meat well with this mixture, working it
   into the cuts.
3. Place the meat in the roasting pan, place the onion slices on
   top of the meat, cover the pan with plastic wrap, and refrigerate the pork for at least 24 hours.
4. Remove the plastic wrap and bake the pork at 350° for 4
   hours. Serve it sliced.

Black Beans
Frijoles Negros

Preparation and cooking time: 2¾ hours, plus overnight soaking of the beans   *Serves 8*

What You Need

1 pound of dried black beans
1 large green pepper, whole, with seeds and membranes removed
1 bay leaf
1 large onion, whole
1 teaspoon of minced garlic
½ cup of dry white wine
1 tablespoon of vinegar
1 cup of olive oil
salt and pepper to taste
4 cups of white rice

large mixing bowl
kitchen knife
cutting board
large, heavy pot with lid
large saucepan with lid
measuring cup
measuring spoons
long mixing spoon

What You Do

1. In the mixing bowl, soak the beans overnight in water twice as deep as the beans. Drain and rinse the beans.
2. Place them in the pot and cover them with water to 1 inch above the level of the beans. Add the green pepper.
3. Bring the beans and pepper to a boil over high heat, then lower the heat and simmer them, covered, for 2 hours.
4. About 10 minutes before the beans and pepper are done, start preparing the rice according to the directions on the package. If you are using instant rice, you can wait until 10 minutes or so before the entire recipe is finished.
5. When the beans and pepper are done, add to them the bay leaf, onion, garlic, wine, and vinegar. Bring the mixture to a boil over high heat, then reduce the heat and simmer, uncovered, for about 20 minutes, stirring often.
6. Stir in the olive oil, salt, and pepper. Serve the beans hot over the rice.

Avocado Salad

Preparation time: 1½ hours *Serves 8*

What You Need

6 ripe avocados	kitchen knife
¼ cup of lemon juice	cutting board
1 teaspoon of salt	medium-sized mixing bowl
lettuce	measuring cup
	measuring spoons
	long mixing spoon
	plastic wrap

What You Do

1. Peel the avocados and cut them into bite-sized pieces. Discard the pits. Place the avocado pieces in the bowl.
2. Sprinkle them with the lemon juice and salt. Stir the mixture gently to coat the avocados.
3. Put the bowl, covered with plastic wrap, in the refrigerator for 1 hour. Stir the mixture at least once during this time.
4. Serve the chilled salad on individual plates lined with lettuce.

Denmark

My mother's parents came to the United States from Denmark immediately after they were married in 1931. They settled and started farming in southwestern Iowa, where they still live. My mother, who was born in Iowa, spoke Danish before she spoke English. She had to learn English before starting school.

Now our family, which includes me, my three brothers, and one sister, lives in Albion, Nebraska. When I was eight years old, we all went to Denmark to visit my great-grandfather and great-grandmother, great-aunts and uncles, and lots of my mother's cousins. We were there one month, and I learned some Danish words. I'm looking forward to going to Denmark again someday.

My favorite interests are playing the piano, stamp collecting, and model rocketry. I also do some cooking. I hope you'll enjoy my Danish recipes as much as our family does. Everyone loves Danish Meatballs, which are good for dinner or as a party snack. The Flour Dumplings are great with any kind of soup, and Apple Dessert is a traditional dessert served at Christmas in Denmark.

Robert Fox, 13

Danish Meatballs
Frikadeller

Preparation and cooking time: about 1½ hours, plus 3 hours of refrigeration

Serves 8

What You Need

1 egg
1½ pounds of ground beef
¾ pound of ground pork
1 teaspoon of salt
¼ teaspoon of allspice
¼ teaspoon of pepper
½ medium-sized onion
1 13-ounce can of evaporated milk
2 tablespoons of flour
½ cup of dried bread or cracker crumbs
½ cup of water
3 tablespoons of oil

wire whisk or fork
small mixing bowl
kitchen knife
cutting board
measuring spoons
large mixing bowl
measuring cup
plastic wrap
large frying pan
long mixing spoon
baking dish with lid

What You Do

1. With the wire whisk or fork, beat the egg in the small bowl.
2. Mince the onion and mix it with the beef, pork, egg, salt, allspice, and pepper in the large bowl.
3. Gradually add the milk, then the flour, then the crumbs, stirring between each addition.
4. Blend in the water. Stir until the mixture is thoroughly moistened and sticky. Cover the bowl with plastic wrap and refrigerate for at least 3 hours.
5. Form the mixture into 2-inch balls. (If you are planning to serve the meatballs at a party, make the balls smaller, so they will be easy to eat on a toothpick.)
6. Preheat the oven to 300°.
7. Heat the oil in the frying pan over medium heat and brown the meatballs on all sides.
8. Remove them from the pan and put them in one layer in the baking dish. Cover the dish and bake for about 20 minutes.

Flour Dumplings
Melboller

Preparation and cooking time: ¾ hour *Serves 4*

What You Need

4 tablespoons of butter or margarine	measuring spoons
¾ cup of flour	medium-sized saucepan
1¼ cups of water	measuring cup
2 eggs	long mixing spoon
1 tablespoon of sugar	large saucepan with lid
½ teaspoon of salt	teaspoon
6–8 cups of chicken broth	slotted spoon
	serving bowl

What You Do

1. Melt the butter or margarine in the smaller saucepan over medium heat. Add the flour, stirring continuously until well mixed.
2. Add the water and keep stirring until the mixture easily pulls away from the spoon and the sides of the pan. Cool for 10 minutes.
3. Add the eggs, beating well after each one. Stir in the sugar and salt.
4. In the large saucepan, bring the broth to a boil.
5. Dip the teaspoon into water and then into the batter (this will prevent the batter from sticking to the spoon). Drop a spoonful of batter into the boiling broth. Continue doing this until you have enough dumplings to cover the surface of the broth. The dumplings should be barely touching. Cover the pot, reduce the heat to low, and simmer for 2 minutes. Turn the dumplings and cook them, covered, 2 minutes longer.
6. Using the slotted spoon, remove the dumplings from the boiling liquid to the serving bowl and pour the broth over them. Serve in individual bowls.

Apple Dessert
Ablekage

Preparation and cooking time: about 2 hours   *Serves 6*

What You Need

7–8 medium-sized cooking
    apples
¼ cup of water
1 cup of sugar
1 teaspoon of vanilla
½ cup of butter or mar-
    garine
2 cups of dry bread
    crumbs
2 tablespoons of sugar
whipped cream (see
    "Whipping Cream,"
    p. 8)

vegetable peeler
kitchen knife
cutting board
measuring spoons
measuring cup
large saucepan with lid
long mixing spoon
large frying pan
medium-sized serving bowl

What You Do

1. Peel, core, and slice the apples into ¼-inch-thick slices. Put the slices and water into the saucepan. Cover and cook over medium heat for 2 minutes.
2. Add the cup of sugar, reduce heat, stir gently, and let the mixture simmer, uncovered, for 5 minutes, stirring occasionally. Drain off any juice. Cool the apples. Stir in the vanilla.
3. Melt the butter or margarine in the frying pan over low heat. Add the bread crumbs and the 2 tablespoons of sugar. Cook, stirring frequently, until the bread crumbs are browned. Cool.
4. Layer the apples and the crumb mixture in the serving bowl, starting and ending with apples. Chill the dessert for at least 1 hour.
5. Top with whipped cream or ice cream and serve.

Equatorial Guinea

I am from Equatorial Guinea, formerly Spanish Guinea, on the west coast of Africa. Equatorial Guinea is a small country, about as large as the state of Maryland. It has a few more than 310,000 people, about the same number as in Miami, Florida. The country has two provinces. One is Rio Muni, on the continent of Africa. The other is an island, Fernando Po. Fernando Po is where I come from. The people on Fernando Po are among the most prosperous in all Africa. Most of them are small farm owners, as my parents were before we came to the United States.

Two main groups of people live on Fernando Po, the Bubis and the Fernandinos. The Bubis were there when the first Portuguese ships arrived in 1472. The Fernandinos, descendants of Africans freed from slave ships, were brought to the island by the British in the late 1800s.

Because Equatorial Guinea was once owned by Spain (it got its independence in 1968), there is a lot of Spanish influence in the country. Spanish is spoken everywhere, along with African languages. In the cities, people eat both Spanish and African food. But in the country, most people eat African food only. The food I like best is African.

Adolpho Obiang, 19

Grilled Fish
Djom

Preparation and cooking time: 1¼ hours   *Serves 4*

What You Need

banana leaves or alumi-
  num foil
4 fish fillets (about 2
  pounds), such as had-
  dock, cod, or flounder
¼ teaspoon of garlic pow-
  der
¼ teaspoon of onion pow-
  der
½ teaspoon of salt
1 red pepper, cut into ¼-
  inch strips
3 tablespoons of lemon
  juice

outdoor grill (optional)
charcoal briquets (op-
  tional)
measuring spoons
kitchen knife
cutting board
string (optional)

What You Do

1. Heat a bed of charcoal briquets until they turn white. If in-
   doors, preheat the oven to 375°.
2. If you are using banana leaves, soften them by placing them
   near the heat of the grill or on top of the heated stove.
3. Place each fish fillet on a banana leaf or a piece of aluminum
   foil. Sprinkle some garlic powder, onion powder, and salt on
   the fillet. Place some red pepper strips on the fish and sprinkle
   on some lemon juice.
4. Wrap the fish tightly in the banana leaf or foil. You will have
   to tie the banana leaf with wet string.
5. Put the wrapped fillets on the coals or on a rack in the oven.
   Cook until done: about 45 minutes over the coals; 30 minutes
   in the oven.
6. Serve the fish on plates in their wrappers. But don't eat the banana leaves!

Meat Stew
Ogwono

Preparation and cooking time: about 2¼ hours   *Serves 3–4*

What You Need

1 pound of beef, lamb, or veal, cut into 2-inch cubes

1 cup of cold water ·

3 fresh tomatoes, cut into pieces, or 1 cup of canned tomatoes, drained

2 large onions, chopped

1 clove of garlic, minced

1 teaspoon of salt

½ teaspoon of pepper

½ cup of peanut butter

1½–2 cups of white rice

kitchen knife

cutting board

measuring cup

measuring spoons

large, heavy pot with lid

long mixing spoon

large saucepan with lid

What You Do

1. Combine the meat, water, tomatoes, onion, garlic, salt, and pepper in the pot. Cover and bring the mixture to a boil over high heat.
2. Lower the heat and simmer the mixture, covered, for 1½ hours, or until the meat is tender. Add water if needed as the mixture simmers.
3. When the stew has cooked 1 hour, you can start preparing the rice according to the directions on the package. If you are using instant rice, wait until the stew has been cooking 1 hour and 20 minutes.
4. When the stew is done, add the peanut butter, stirring constantly to prevent sticking. Serve the stew over the rice.

Pepper Soup

Preparation and cooking time: about 1½ hours   *Serves 4–6*

What You Need

1½ cups of cold water
1½ cups of fish (red snap-
   per, flounder, or fresh
   tuna) cut into bite-sized
   pieces
3 large onions, thinly sliced
1 green tomato, quartered
1 large green pepper, seeded
   and chopped
1 teaspoon of salt
½ teaspoon of pepper
½ teaspoon of paprika
juice of 1 lemon, or 3 tablespoons of bottled lemon
   juice
cooking oil

measuring cup
large, heavy pot with lid
kitchen knife
cutting board
measuring spoons
lemon squeezer
long mixing spoon

What You Do

1. Bring the water to a boil in the pot.
2. Add all the ingredients except the cooking oil. Cover the pot
   and cook over very low heat for 1 hour, stirring occasionally.
   Add a little water if the mixture seems to be drying out.
3. Add 3 or 4 drops of cooking oil, cook for 3 minutes more, and
   serve hot in individual bowls.

France

My father was born in the heart of Acadiana, an area of southern Louisiana settled originally by French Acadians who were exiled from Nova Scotia in the mid-eighteenth century. In Acadiana our family name is pronounced "Ree-SHARD," and my relatives all speak French daily.

Acadiana is famous for its "Cajun" French cooking, including spicy seafood and rich dishes with sauces. Our family enjoys seafood in sauces where we now live, on the Florida Gulf Coast. In fact, my brother and I go snorkeling for scallops every August, and Dad cooks the meat from them in a sauce.

French chefs are world famous, and Acadian men are all good cooks, too. I prepare the traditional Sunday breakfast at our house: Pain Perdu (Lost Bread), a favorite adapted by Americans, who serve it with syrup and call it French toast. More unusual for breakfast are Calas, or Egg and Rice Cakes, which also make good snacks. One of our dessert favorites is Strawberries Chantilly (named for a small town near Paris, also known for its lace).

Greg Richard, 15

Lost Bread
Pain Perdu

What You Need

2 eggs
1 cup of milk
1 heaping tablespoon of
  sugar
½ teaspoon of vanilla
2 tablespoons of butter or
  margarine
6 slices of stale white
  bread
cinnamon
nutmeg

wide, shallow dish
wire whisk
measuring cup
measuring spoons
large frying pan
spatula

What You Do

1. With a wire whisk, beat the eggs in the dish. Add the milk and sugar, and stir until the sugar is dissolved. Stir in the vanilla.
2. Dip each slice of bread into the egg mixture. Allow the bread to absorb the milk but not to become soggy.
3. Heat the butter or margarine in the frying pan over medium high heat until it is very hot. Then place the bread slices in the pan and fry them until they are golden brown, turning once or twice as necessary.
4. Remove the bread from the pan. Sprinkle each piece with cinnamon and nutmeg before serving.

Egg and Rice Cakes
Calas

CAUTION!
THIS RECIPE CALLS FOR FRYING IN DEEP FAT.
DO NOT GO AHEAD UNTIL YOU READ PAGE 7.

Preparation and cooking time: about ½ hour

Makes 18–20 cakes

What You Need

1 cup of rice
3 eggs
¼ teaspoon of vanilla
½ teaspoon of nutmeg
½ cup of sugar
6 tablespoons of flour
½ teaspoon of salt
3 teaspoons of baking powder
oil for frying
confectioners' sugar

saucepan with lid
large mixing bowl
egg beater or wire whisk
measuring spoons
long mixing spoon
flour sifter
electric deep-fat fryer
paper towels

What You Do

1. Cook the rice according to the directions on the package.
2. In the bowl, beat together the eggs, vanilla, and nutmeg. Stir in the cooked rice.
3. Put the sugar, flour, salt, and baking powder into the flour sifter and sift into the rice and egg mixture. Blend thoroughly.
4. Pour about 2 inches of oil into the fryer and heat to the temperature recommended by the manufacturer. Drop the batter by spoonfuls into the oil and fry the cakes until they are golden brown (about 1 minute).
5. Drain the cakes on paper towels. Sprinkle them with confectioners' sugar and serve them right away as dessert or as a treat.

Strawberries Chantilly
Fraises Chantilly

Preparation time: about 1 hour   *Serves 6*

What You Need

1 quart of fresh strawberries
2 tablespoons of light Karo
   syrup
2 egg whites (see "Separating Eggs," p. 7)
4 tablespoons of confec-
   tioners' sugar
whipped cream (see
   "Whipping Cream,"
   p. 8)

kitchen knife
cutting board
medium-sized mixing bowl
measuring spoons
long mixing spoon
small mixing bowl, chilled
egg beater or wire whisk,
   chilled

What You Do

1. Wash and remove the stems from the strawberries. Cut each berry in half.
2. Place the berries in the medium-sized mixing bowl. Add the Karo syrup and stir gently until the berries are coated. Place the bowl in the refrigerator until the berries are well chilled (about 30 minutes).
3. Using the egg beater, beat the egg whites in the small mixing bowl until they are white and stiff. Gradually add the confectioners' sugar while beating the egg whites constantly.
4. Fold the egg-white mixture into the chilled strawberries. Refrigerate until serving time.
5. Top each portion of strawberries with whipped cream and serve.

Germany

Having been brought up in a German home (my grandparents on both sides came from Germany), I am very fond of German cooking. Among my other favorite things are my German boxer, my ten-speed bike, and tennis.

My family has lived in many places — Iowa, New York, Massachusetts, and now Phoenix, Arizona — but no matter where we live, our holiday celebrations are always influenced by old German customs. And that means lots of good German food. Many of the recipes are now well known in the United States, such as Stollen, the fruited Christmas bread. However, here are some recipes I would like to share that are for more than one occasion. For example, the German Filled Pancakes can be a dessert, a breakfast dish, or a snack in front of the fire.

Mark Tondat, 15

German Filled Pancakes
Pfannkuchen

Preparation and cooking time: about ¾ hour   *Serves 4*

What You Need

1 cup of *sifted* flour (see p. 4)
1½ teaspoons of sugar
½ teaspoon of salt
1 egg
1 cup of milk
½ teaspoon of vanilla
3 tablespoons of butter or margarine
jam
sour cream or confectioners' sugar

flour sifter
measuring cup
measuring spoons
large mixing bowl
medium-sized mixing bowl
fork or wire whisk
wooden spoon
large frying pan
spatula

What You Do

1. Sift together into the large bowl the sifted flour, sugar, and salt.
2. Beat the egg, milk, and vanilla together in the smaller bowl and add to the flour mixture. Mix thoroughly.
3. Heat the butter or margarine in the frying pan over medium heat until it sizzles. Drop the flour mixture by spoonfuls into the pan and fry the pancakes until they are golden brown, turning once. (Lift slightly with the spatula to tell when to turn them.) Repeat until all the batter is used, adding more butter to the pan if necessary. The pancakes should be about 4 inches in diameter.
4. Spread the pancakes with your favorite jam and roll them up. Top with sour cream or confectioners' sugar and serve.

Hot Potato Salad with Bacon
Warmer Kartoffelsalat mit Speck

Preparation and cooking time: about 1½ hours   *Serves 2–4*

What You Need

3 medium-sized potatoes	vegetable brush
6 slices of bacon, diced	medium-sized saucepan
1 medium onion, diced	with lid
½ cup of vinegar	vegetable peeler
½ cup of beef bouillon	kitchen knife
1 teaspoon of salt	cutting board
1 teaspoon of pepper	serving bowl
1 teaspoon of sugar	large frying pan
1 egg yolk (see "Separating	measuring spoons
Eggs," p. 7)	long mixing spoon
	small mixing bowl
	wire whisk or fork

What You Do

1. Scrub the potatoes with the vegetable brush, rinse them, and put them in the saucepan. Cover them with water, put on the lid, and bring the water to a boil over high heat. Turn the heat to low and simmer the potatoes about 30 minutes, or until they are tender. Drain them and let them cool.
2. Peel the potatoes and cut them into ¼-inch slices. Place them in the serving bowl.
3. Cook the bacon in the frying pan over medium heat until it is almost crisp. Add the onion and cook the mixture, stirring, until the onion is soft and the bacon crisp.
4. Add the vinegar, bouillon, and seasonings to the pan. Stir and let the mixture come to a boil.
5. Beat the egg yolk in the small bowl with the wire whisk and stir it into the sauce. Remove the sauce from the heat. Pour it over the potatoes and mix gently. Serve the salad hot or cold.

Great Britain

My mother was born and brought up in England. She married my father, and they moved to the United States, where my sister was born. A year later they moved back to England, where I was born. I have lived over half my life there.

Now we live in Florida, where I am a senior in high school. Since I usually work during the summer and the school year to make money, I don't have as much time to cook as I might like.

Many people think that English cooking is boring and unimaginative. That's not true! Trifle, a dessert with cream and pudding, is a favorite at our house, and all my friends love it. Although it looks hard, Trifle is really quite easy to make. It is also delicious the next day, *if* there is any left over. Steak and Mushroom Pie, like all kinds of meat pies, is very popular in England. It is especially nice on a cold winter night.

Jacqueline Hendrix, 16

Steak and Mushroom Pie

Preparation and cooking time: 3½ hours   *Serves 6*

What You Need

FOR THE PASTRY

1 cup of butter or margarine
1½ cups of all-purpose flour
pinch of salt
2 tablespoons of cold water

FOR THE FILLING

1½ pounds of lean stew beef, cut into ½-inch cubes
¼ cup of flour
¾ teaspoon of salt
¼ teaspoon of pepper
1 large onion, sliced
1 tablespoon of flour
½ pound of mushrooms, cleaned and stems removed (see p. 8)
2 tablespoons of oil
½ cup of beef stock (canned or made from a bouillon cube)

measuring cup
kitchen knife
cutting board
medium-sized mixing bowl
wooden spoon
measuring spoons
waxed paper
rolling pin
9-inch pie plate
pastry brush
paper bag
plate
large frying pan with lid
long mixing spoon

What You Do

MAKE THE PASTRY (STEPS 1–4)

1. Cut the butter or margarine into little squares and put them in the mixing bowl.
2. Add the flour and salt, and mix with the wooden spoon, pressing against the sides of the bowl, until the mixture resembles fine bread crumbs.
3. Mix in the cold water. Form the dough into a ball.
4. Divide the pastry in half. Wrap each half in waxed paper and put in the refrigerator.

MAKE AND COOK THE FILLING (STEPS 5–9)

5. Remove all fat and gristle from the meat.
6. Put the flour, salt, and pepper into a paper bag. Add the beef cubes to the bag, close it tightly, and shake it to coat the beef with the seasoned flour. Remove the beef and set the cubes aside on the plate.
7. Coat the onion slices in the same way.
8. Heat the oil in the frying pan over medium heat, and fry the onions and mushroom caps until the onions begin to soften. Add the meat and fry until the cubes are golden brown, turning them to brown on all sides.
9. Add the 1 tablespoon of flour to the pan and gradually blend in the beef stock. Gently bring the mixture to a boil, still over medium heat, stirring constantly. Cover the pan, turn the heat to low, and simmer the mixture for 1½ hours, or until the meat is tender.

MAKE AND BAKE THE PIE (STEPS 10–14)

10. Preheat the oven to 400°.
11. Remove half the dough from the refrigerator. Flour the rolling pin and cutting board, and roll the dough into a 10-inch circle. Line the pie plate with the rolled-out circle.
12. Spoon the meat mixture into the pastry shell.
13. Roll out the other half of the dough as described in Step 11 and place it on top of the pie. Pinch the edges of both pieces together to seal them.
14. Cut 2 or 3 slits in the top of the pastry. Bake for 30 minutes or until the pie is golden brown.

Trifle

Preparation and refrigeration time: about 3 hours   *Serves 10*

What You Need

2-layer sponge cake or 2
   packages of ladyfingers
jam (your favorite flavor)
2 packages of vanilla pudding (not instant)
5 cups of milk
2 cups of fruit, such as bananas, strawberries, or
   cherries, fresh or canned,
   cut into bite-sized pieces
   (optional)
1 package of red or green
   gelatin dessert
2½ cups of water
1 cup of whipping cream
fruit and nuts for garnish
   (optional)

kitchen knife
cutting board
measuring cup
large saucepan
large serving bowl (clear
   glass is best)
large mixing bowl
medium-sized mixing bowl
egg beater or wire whisk

What You Do

1. Thinly spread the jam on each layer of cake. Slice the cake into
   1-inch squares. If using ladyfingers, spread each with jam and
   slice into thirds.
2. Prepare the vanilla pudding according to the directions on the
   package, but add 5 cups of milk instead of the 4 cups called
   for. Cool slightly.
3. Put enough cake pieces into the serving bowl to line the bottom. Cover the cake pieces with a layer of pudding; then add
   some fruit if you wish. Repeat the layers until all the pudding
   has been used, ending with pudding (or fruit, if used). Put the
   bowl in the refrigerator.

4. Prepare the gelatin according to the directions on the package, but add an extra ½ cup of water (2½ cups in all). Put the gelatin in the refrigerator until it starts to set slightly (about 15 minutes). Pour it over the layers of cake and pudding; the gelatin should seep through the layers. Refrigerate the pudding until the gelatin has completely set (about 1 hour).
5. Half an hour before the pudding is ready, refrigerate the medium-sized bowl and the egg beater. At serving time, whip the cream in the chilled bowl (see the instructions on p. 8), spread it on the trifle, and garnish with fruits and nuts.

Greece

My grandparents and my father came to the United States from Greece. My mother was born in Niagara Falls, New York, and is a United States citizen. Although my two brothers and I were also born in the United States, we have been brought up with the Greek beliefs and traditions.

My grandparents have been in the restaurant business for thirty years and have three restaurants in Niagara Falls. Everyone in my family helps out in the restaurants. My father is a co-owner and also a bartender. My mother is a hostess, and one of my brothers is a chef. My other brother works with my uncle as co-owner of another restaurant.

Every Easter all of our relatives and our family go to my grand-mother's house for dinner. We have one of my favorites, Lamb with Rice, which is traditional at Eastertime, Greek Salad, and delicious Shortbread Cookies baked by my grandmother. They are all easy to make — and delicious to eat!

Tina Churakos, 15

Lamb with Rice
Arni me Rizi

Preparation and cooking time: ¾ hour   *Serves 4*

What You Need

¼ cup of butter or mar-
  garine
½ cup of chopped onion
1½ cups of long-grain
  white rice
3 cups of boiling water
3 chicken bouillon cubes
1 teaspoon of dried mint
2 cups of cooked roast
  lamb, cut into 1-inch
  cubes
2 tablespoons of chopped
  parsley

measuring cup
kitchen knife
cutting board
large saucepan with lid
long mixing spoon
measuring spoons

What You Do

1. Melt the butter or margarine in the saucepan over low heat. Add the onions and cook them until they are limp, stirring occasionally.
2. Add the rice and mix well. Cover the saucepan and cook the mixture for 5 minutes.
3. Add the boiling water, bouillon cubes, and mint. Simmer 4 or 5 minutes, stirring often.
4. Add the lamb cubes. Mix well. Continue cooking, uncovered, for 5 minutes or until all the liquid is absorbed. Transfer to a serving dish, garnish with the parsley, and serve.

Greek Salad
Salata

Preparation time: ½ hour (dressing must be refrigerated for several hours)   *Serves 4–6*

What You Need

FOR THE DRESSING

2 cups of olive oil
1 cup of lemon juice
1 teaspoon of oregano
½ clove of garlic, diced
1 teaspoon of salt
½ teaspoon of pepper
5 or 6 celery leaves,
   chopped

FOR THE SALAD

4 tomatoes, cut into
   wedges
1 cucumber, thinly sliced
3 onions, thinly sliced
¼ pound of feta cheese,
   cut in small pieces
½ cup of Greek olives

kitchen knife
cutting board
measuring cup
measuring spoons
mixing bowl or glass jar
   with lid
salad bowl
salad fork and spoon

What You Do

1. Combine all the dressing ingredients in the mixing bowl or jar. For more flavor, let the dressing sit in the refrigerator for several hours before using it.
2. In the salad bowl, combine the tomatoes, cucumber, and onion. Stir or shake the salad dressing to mix it well and pour on just enough to moisten the vegetables. Toss. Arrange the olives and cheese on top of the salad and serve.

Shortbread Cookies
Kourambiedes

Preparation and cooking time: about 1½ hours (dough must be refrigerated for an additional 2 hours)

Makes about 4 dozen cookies

What You Need

2 sticks of sweet butter, at room temperature
½ cup of confectioners' sugar
1 egg yolk (see "Separating Eggs," p. 7)
½ teaspoon of vanilla
2¼ cups of all-purpose flour
1 teaspoon of baking powder
½ cup of walnuts, finely chopped
additional confectioners' sugar

large mixing bowl
electric mixer or wire whisk
measuring cup
flour sifter
wooden spoon
measuring spoons
kitchen knife
medium-sized mixing bowl
plastic wrap
baking sheet

What You Do

1. Place the softened butter in the large mixing bowl and beat it with an electric mixer or wire whisk until it is light and fluffy.
2. Sift the sugar into the butter. Cream them together with the wooden spoon. Add the egg yolk and vanilla. Mix well.
3. Into the other bowl, sift the flour and baking powder together. Mix in the nuts. Add to the butter-sugar mixture about ¼ cup at a time. Mix well after each addition.
4. Mix the ingredients to form a soft dough. Cover the bowl with plastic wrap and place it in the refrigerator for 2 hours.
5. Preheat the oven to 350°.
6. On a lightly floured surface, roll 2 tablespoons of dough at a time into a small ball, using the palm of your hand. (Lightly

flour your hand if the dough sticks.) Place the balls on the ungreased baking sheet, about 2 inches apart, and bake them for 15 to 20 minutes, until they are golden brown.

7. Spread some confectioners' sugar on a piece of waxed paper and roll the cookies in the sugar while they are still hot.

Hungary

My great-grandfather was born in Budapest, Hungary, in the late 1800s and came to America when he was very young. After fighting in World War I, he went to work for *Life* magazine and eventually became one of the owners. Of course, I never had a chance to meet my great-grandfather, but I've learned a lot about him from my grandmother.

Hungarian people love good food and happy music, and great-grandfather was no exception. If there is such a thing as a national dish in Hungary, it would have to be Goulash, which was one of great-grandfather's favorites. There is definitely a national spice in Hungary, and that's paprika, a powder made from sweet red peppers. In this country, paprika is mild in taste, but in Hungary it can be either sweet or hot. Hungarians use it in just about everything. When you make Goulash, you should try to use Hungarian paprika, but if you can't find it, regular paprika will do.

Hungary is also noted for its pastries, which, like most pastries, are very rich. Apricot Pastries are fun to make, and they taste delicious.

Peter Sliker, 15

Hungarian Goulash
Gulyás

What You Need

4 tablespoons of olive oil
3 or 4 yellow onions, diced
2 pounds of stew beef, cut
   into 1-inch cubes
1 small can of tomato
   paste
½ cup of water
1 tablespoon of Hungarian
   paprika (or 1½ table-
   spoons of regular pa-
   prika)
1 pound of wide noodles,
   cooked according to the
   directions on the package

measuring spoons
large frying pan with lid
large kitchen knife
cutting board
long mixing spoon
measuring cup

What You Do

1. Put the oil in the frying pan and heat it over medium-low heat for about 2 minutes.
2. Add the onions and cook them, stirring occasionally, until they start to turn brown around the edges.
3. Add the beef cubes and cook them, turning occasionally, until all the red is gone.
4. Add the remaining ingredients (except the noodles) and stir to combine them.
5. Cover the pan and simmer the goulash for about 2 hours, or until the meat is tender. If the meat sticks during cooking, add a little more water. Serve the goulash over the noodles.

Apricot Pastries

Preparation and cooking time: about 1½ hours (dough must be refrigerated for an additional 2 hours)

Makes 4 dozen pastries

What You Need

1 pound of unsalted butter, at room temperature
1 pound of cream cheese, at room temperature
2 cups of sifted flour
apricot jam

large mixing bowl
wooden spoon
measuring cup
flour sifter
waxed paper
cutting board
rolling pin
kitchen knife
baking sheet
wire rack

What You Do

1. Using the wooden spoon, cream the butter and cream cheese together in the mixing bowl.
2. Gradually stir the flour into the mixture, about ¼ cup at a time. Mix well after each addition.
3. Divide the dough into four balls of equal size, wrap each in a piece of waxed paper, and refrigerate them for at least 2 hours.
4. Preheat the oven to 400°.
5. Flour the cutting board and rolling pin. Roll out one ball of dough until it is about half an inch thick.
6. Cut the dough into 2-inch strips and the strips into 2-inch squares. Put about 1 teaspoonful of jam in the center of each square, fold the dough in half, and pinch the edges together.
7. Repeat this procedure with the remaining balls of dough.
8. Put the pastries on the baking sheet about 1 inch apart and bake them for 20 minutes, or until golden brown. (It may be necessary to bake the pastries in more than one batch, depending on the size of your baking sheet.)
9. Cool the pastries on a wire rack before serving.

Ireland

Ní geal an gáire ach san aít a mbíonnan biadh! In Gaelic, that means "laughter is the gayest where the food is best!" Our family came from Dublin, Ireland. My parents lived there for most of their young lives, so I'm a direct Irish descendant. Although my name is quite common in Ireland, most people in this country have trouble pronouncing it at first. It sounds like this: Shi-VAHN.

I was born in Toledo, Ohio, but soon after, we moved to Boston. I have two brothers and one sister, but I'm the oldest. My father is an orthopedic surgeon, and my mother is a mother.

Most Irish foods are plain, but very enjoyable and hearty. They're filling, too. Many Irish families have gardens in their backyards, so they have plenty of fresh vegetables. Fresh fish is also very popular in Ireland.

The following recipes are really good and easy, so go ahead and try them. Irish Soda Bread has been around for hundreds of years and is a favorite in every Irish home (including ours). Dublin Coddle is straight from my grandmother's kitchen. It may sound and look awful, but looks can be very deceiving. It's wonderful on a cold night, and tastes great with Irish Soda Bread. My parents love Irish coffee, so as a treat, we have it, kids' style.

Siobahn O'Riordan, 13

Dublin Coddle

Preparation and cooking time: ¾ hour   *Serves 3–4*

What You Need

6 medium-sized onions
½ pound of sliced bacon
1 pound of pork sausage
¼ teaspoon of pepper
½ cup of water

kitchen knife
cutting board
measuring cup
measuring spoons
large frying pan with lid
long mixing spoon

What You Do

1. Thinly slice the onions. Cut the bacon slices into 1-inch-long pieces.
2. Put all the ingredients in the frying pan and simmer them gently over low heat for 30 minutes, covered. Stir the mixture occasionally to make sure the meat cooks evenly.
3. Serve hot with Irish Soda Bread (see the next recipe).

Irish Soda Bread

Preparation and baking time: 1¼ hours   *Serves 6*

What You Need

4 cups of all-purpose flour
1 teaspoon of baking soda
1 teaspoon of salt
1–1½ cups of buttermilk
butter or margarine

large mixing bowl
measuring cup
measuring spoons
flour sifter
long mixing spoon
cutting board
baking sheet
small knife

What You Do

1. Preheat the oven to 425°.
2. Put the flour, baking soda, and salt together into the sifter and sift them into the mixing bowl. Gradually add 1 cup of buttermilk, stirring constantly. Mix until the ingredients form a dough.
3. Put the dough on a lightly floured board and shape it into a flat round loaf, about 8 inches across and 1½ inches high.
4. Grease the baking sheet with the butter or margarine. Put the loaf on the baking sheet and with the knife, cut an X, half an inch deep, into the top of the dough.
5. Bake the bread in the center of the oven for 45 minutes. Serve at once, cut into slices.

Irish Coffee for Kids

Preparation time: 10 minutes

Serves 1

What You Need

1 cup of boiling water
1 teaspoon of instant coffee
1 tablespoon of brown sugar
prepared whipped topping

teakettle or small saucepan
measuring cup
heat-proof cup
stemmed glass
measuring spoons
metal spoon

What You Do

1. In the teakettle bring 1 cup of water to a boil. Put the coffee into the heat-proof cup and add the boiling water. Stir.
2. Put the sugar in the stemmed glass. Put the metal spoon in the glass (to prevent the glass from cracking) and pour in the hot coffee. Stir very well.
3. Add a dollop of whipped topping and serve immediately.

Israel

I was the first American citizen in my family because I was born in the United States when my Israeli parents were visiting here. Even though I was just a tiny baby and couldn't sign my name, I was given my own passport. Later, my father, my mother, my older brother, and my older sister also became American citizens. We live in Boston now, but we still go back to Israel for visits. My father is a physicist, and my mother is an artist. We speak Hebrew at home, and we often eat Israeli foods.

Israeli recipes are a mixture of Jewish specialties from the Middle East and from Eastern Europe. Most of the people in Israel first came from those lands. Of course, the recipes were changed from their original versions to take into account the hot climate and the kinds of food people could get in Israel.

Some of the recipes are very hot and spicy. They take getting used to. (I once served my friends a spicy dish called felafel, and they decided it should be called "feel-awful"!) Other recipes are cool and refreshing, like Marak Perot Kar (Fruit Soup), or moist and sweet, like Kugel Itriot (Sweet Noodle Pudding). Even my native American friends can't resist them.

Tamar Amir, 16

Fruit Soup
Marak Perot Kar

Preparation and cooking time: 1¾ hours (soup must be refrigerated for an additional 2 hours)　　*Serves 4–6*

What You Need

1 small cantaloupe
about 1½ pounds of mixed
　fresh fruits, such as
　pears, plums, peaches,
　apricots, strawberries,
　grapes, cherries
2 medium-sized apples
½ cup of lemon juice
¼ cup of sugar
water
¾ cup of orange juice
whipped cream (see
　"Whipping Cream,"
　p. 8), sour cream, or ice
　cream

teakettle or saucepan
kitchen knife
cutting board
large pot with lid
long mixing spoon
food mill or sieve and
　large mixing bowl

What You Do

1. Fill the teakettle or saucepan with water and bring to a boil over high heat.
2. Cut the cantaloupe in half. Remove and discard the seeds and fibers. Scoop out the pulp and chop it coarsely.
3. Wash the rest of the fruit. Peel the large fruit, such as apples, pears, and peaches, and coarsely chop them. Throw away any seeds.
4. Put the fruit, half the lemon juice, and the sugar into the pot. Add enough boiling water to cover the fruit by 1 inch. Put on the lid, bring the water to a boil over high heat, turn the heat to low, and simmer until the fruit is soft, about 30 minutes.
5. Puree the fruit by putting it through the food mill. (Or pour it into a sieve set over the mixing bowl; press the fruit through the sieve with the back of a spoon.)

6. Stir the rest of the lemon juice and the orange juice into the soup and mix well. Refrigerate the soup, uncovered, for at least 2 hours.
7. Serve the soup in small bowls, topped with whipped cream, sour cream, or ice cream.

Sweet Noodle Pudding
Kugel Itriot

Preparation and baking time: 1¾ hours   *Serves 6*

What You Need

½ pound of noodles
3 eggs
¼ cup of sugar
8 ounces of sour cream
8 ounces of cottage cheese
1 teaspoon of vanilla
½ teaspoon of ground cin-
   namon
¾ cup of raisins (or a combination of raisins,
   chopped apples,
   peaches, dried fruit, almonds)
butter or margarine

large pot with lid
colander or sieve
large mixing bowl
egg beater
measuring cup
measuring spoons
kitchen knife
long mixing spoon
2-quart casserole

What You Do

1. Preheat the oven to 350°.
2. Cook the noodles according to the directions on the package and drain them.
3. Beat the eggs in the mixing bowl.
4. Add the sugar, sour cream, cottage cheese, vanilla, cinnamon, and fruit, and mix well. Then carefully fold in the noodles.
5. Grease the casserole with butter or margarine. Pour in the mixture and bake uncovered for 1 hour, or until the pudding is firm and the top is light brown. Serve either hot or cold, as part of the main course or as a dessert.

Italy

My grandfather came to the United States from Rome when he was eighteen. He is ninety-one now. Since he had been a bookbinder in Italy, he went to work in a small bookbinding shop in Boston. All his bookbinding was handcrafted.

Grandma came to the United States from Milan with her younger brothers and sisters when she was fourteen. Her mother had just died, so Grandma had to learn to cook because she was the oldest.

I loved to go to Grandma's house. It always smelled of homemade goodies. We always stayed for dinner. Grandma often cooked one of my favorite dishes, Gulnio Milanese — fried chicken Milan-style. That is one recipe Grandma knew I liked. She would tell me, "With a little practice and a sharp knife, anyone can learn to bone a chicken." If you are careful, of course! Anyway, you can always buy it already boned.

Grandma pounded the chicken on her wooden cutting board with her big rolling pin. She made it look so easy. If you were good, she would let you dip the chicken in the bread crumbs. My younger sister and I loved to help her. She served the chicken with potatoes and an Italian salad. The grownups would have wine, and the wine was always homemade.

Like most Italian families, we eat lots of pasta. Besides spaghetti, pasta comes in hundreds of different shapes, which we eat slightly chewy, or *al dente*. Grandma always made her own pasta, but when I make Spaghetti alla Marinara, I buy the spaghetti in a supermarket. Italians eat just a little sauce on their pasta — several tablespoons — instead of the wet, juicy, sauce-covered pasta known here. Serve the spaghetti with crusty Italian bread.

Gail Volpini, 14

Fried Chicken
Gulnio Milanese

Preparation and cooking time: about 1¼ hours   *Serves 4–6*

What You Need

1½ cups of flour
1 cup of Italian bread
  crumbs
2 eggs
3 whole chicken breasts,
  split, skinned, boned,
  and flattened to ¼-inch
  thickness (ask the
  butcher to do this)
½ teaspoon of salt
¼ teaspoon of pepper
2 tablespoons of olive oil
3 tablespoons of butter or
  margarine
1 clove of garlic
lemon quarters

2 plates
measuring cup
shallow bowl
wire whisk or fork
measuring spoons
spatula
large frying pan
paper towels
kitchen knife
cutting board

What You Do

1. Spread the flour on one plate and the bread crumbs on the other.
2. Break the eggs into the bowl and beat them well with the wire whisk.
3. Sprinkle the chicken pieces with salt and pepper, then dust them lightly with the flour. Shake off the excess flour.
4. Dip them in the beaten egg and roll them in the bread crumbs. Press the bread crumbs on the chicken pieces with the palm of your hand to coat them evenly. Shake off the extra crumbs.
5. In the frying pan, heat the oil and the butter or margarine together over medium heat. Fry the garlic clove until it browns lightly, then discard it.
6. Add the chicken three pieces at a time and cook them, turning once, until they are golden brown (about 5–8 minutes on each side).

7. Drain the chicken pieces on paper towels and serve them hot with the lemon quarters. Diners should squeeze lemon juice on the chicken, to taste.

Spaghetti with Tomato Sauce
Spaghetti alla Marinara

Preparation and cooking time: 1¼ hours   *Serves 4–6*

What You Need

2 cloves of garlic
5 or 6 medium-sized toma-
  toes
3 tablespoons of minced
  parsley
¼ cup of olive oil
1¼ teaspoons of salt
½ teaspoon of freshly
  ground black pepper
1 pound of spaghetti
6 quarts (24 cups) of cold
  water
1 tablespoon of oil
2 tablespoons of salt
2 tablespoons of butter or
  margarine
grated Parmesan cheese

kitchen knife
cutting board
large frying pan
measuring cup
measuring spoons
long mixing spoon
6-quart pot with lid
colander
serving dish, heated

What You Do

1. Peel and halve the garlic cloves. Skin the tomatoes (see the instructions on p. 8) and dice them. Mince the parsley.
2. Heat the oil in the frying pan over medium heat, brown the garlic, and then discard it.
3. Add the tomatoes, the 1¼ teaspoons of salt, and the pepper to the pan. Cook over low heat for 20 minutes, or until most of the liquid has evaporated. Mix in the parsley.
4. Put the water in the pot, add the tablespoon of oil and the 2 tablespoons of salt, cover the pot, and bring the water to a fast boil over high heat. Fan the spaghetti in the water, again bring the water to a boil, and cook the spaghetti, uncovered, stirring occasionally to separate the strands. Cook for 7 minutes if using thin spaghetti, longer if the spaghetti is thicker. (Pasta should be slightly chewy.)

5. Drain the spaghetti in the colander and place it in the serving dish. Mix in the butter or margarine.
6. Spoon some of the sauce over the spaghetti and serve it right away. Pass the extra sauce and the grated cheese.

Herbed Zucchini

Preparation and cooking time: ¾ hour

Serves 4

What You Need

1½ pounds of fresh zucchini
½ cup of water
1 clove of garlic, crushed
1 teaspoon of salt
¼ teaspoon of oregano
⅛ teaspoon of basil
¼ teaspoon of marjoram
freshly ground pepper
grated Parmesan cheese

kitchen knife
cutting board
large frying pan with lid
measuring cup
measuring spoons
long mixing spoon

What You Do

1. Wash the zucchini and slice into rounds ¼-inch thick, discarding the ends.
2. Place the rounds in the frying pan with the water, garlic, salt, oregano, basil, marjoram, and pepper. Bring to a boil over high heat.
3. Cover the pan and turn the heat to low. Simmer for about 8 minutes, stirring a few times to blend the flavors.
4. Drain off the water and discard the garlic.
5. Sprinkle the zucchini with Parmesan cheese and serve.

Jamaica

My parents come from Jamaica, West Indies, a small mountainous island in the Caribbean Sea. Jamaica is a little smaller than Connecticut and is only ninety miles south of Cuba. My parents grew up in Kingston, the seaport-capital, during the time the island was still under British rule. (Jamaica became independent in 1962.)

Montego Bay and Ocho Rios are popular resort areas that attract many tourists. Of the 500,000 or so visitors to the country every year, most are American. This tourist trade does much to help the economy.

Typical Jamaican food is hot and spicy, and it takes awhile for Americans to get used to it. The desserts are very sweet, and most are cooked with some form of coconut.

My favorite dinner is Curried Goat with Coconut Rice and Peas, and a glass of ginger beer. (It isn't really beer, but a delicious drink made by fermenting fresh ginger.) If you live near a West Indian market you won't have any trouble finding goat meat, but you can also substitute lamb or beef. Another typical Jamaican dish is Fried Plantains, a fruit that resembles the banana. Plantains aren't good uncooked, but they taste delicious fried.

Pat Isaacs, 18

Curried Goat

Preparation and cooking time: about 2 hours   *Serves 8*

What You Need

4 pounds of fresh goat meat
   (or lamb or beef), cut into
   1-inch cubes
1 tablespoon of curry powder
1 teaspoon of salt
1 teaspoon of black pepper
2 cloves of garlic
2 medium-sized onions,
   chopped
water
4 cups of white rice (op-
   tional)

kitchen knife
cutting board
measuring spoons
4-quart, stove-top casserole
   or large pot with lid

What You Do

1. If using goat meat, rinse the meat with fresh water and drain.
2. Place the meat in the casserole or pot, season it with the curry powder, salt, and pepper, and add the garlic cloves and onion. Add enough water to cover the meat.
3. Bring to a boil over high heat. Reduce the heat to low, cover tightly, and simmer for 1½ hours, or until the meat is tender and the dish has the consistency of stew.
4. About ½ hour before the meat is done, prepare the rice according to the directions on the package. (Instant rice can be prepared just before the meat is done.) Or begin to prepare Coconut Rice and Peas (the next recipe) as soon as the meat is put on the stove to simmer.
5. Serve the meat over mounds of white rice or with Coconut Rice and Peas.

Coconut Rice and Peas

Preparation and cooking time: 2 hours   *Serves 8*

What You Need

1 medium-sized fresh coconut
1½ cups of dried pigeon
  peas or red kidney beans
1 smoked pig tail or 1 large
  smoked ham hock, cut up
  (ask the butcher to do
  this)
2 scallions, chopped
½ teaspoon of thyme
3 cups of water
3 cups of long-grain white
  rice, rinsed

hammer
kitchen knife
grater
small mixing bowl
strainer with fine mesh
cutting board
measuring cup
large pot with lid

What You Do

1. Use the hammer to break open the coconut. Remove the coconut meat with the knife, peel off the brown skin, and rinse the
   meat.
2. Grate the coconut with a hand grater or food processor.
   Squeeze the grated coconut with your hands over the mixing
   bowl to extract the milk. Strain the milk.
3. In the pot, combine the coconut milk, the dried peas or beans,
   and the pig tail or ham hock. Cook the mixture over low heat,
   uncovered, for 1 hour, adding water if it seems dry. The peas or
   beans should be soft, but not broken.
4. Add the scallions, thyme, water, and rice to the pot, and bring
   the mixture to a boil over high heat. Lower the heat and simmer, covered, until the rice is cooked (about 20 minutes). Serve
   the rice with meat, fish, or poultry dishes.

Fried Plantains

Preparation and cooking time: about ½ hour   *Serves 3–4*

What You Need

3–4 firm ripe plantains or
    firm bananas
½ cup of cooking oil

kitchen knife
cutting board
measuring cup
large frying pan
spatula
paper towels

What You Do

1. Peel the plantains and cut them in half, crosswise. Then cut the slices lengthwise, about ¼-inch thick.
2. In the frying pan, heat the oil over medium heat until it sizzles.
3. Fry the plantain slices until they are golden brown on both sides. Turn them once.
4. Drain the slices on paper towels and serve them hot as a snack or with meat, fish, or poultry.

Japan

"Treat food politely," my grandmother says. "If you want to stuff yourself, you must eat somewhere else."

Japanese are very serious and formal about food. When my grandmother cooks for our family, everything has to be just right. The whole meal looks as if it came from an art museum. Not only does my grandmother set the table the way Japanese have been doing for thousands of years, but even the food on the plates is arranged in a special way. "Food is for the spirit as well as the body," Grandmother likes to say.

That may sound as if Japanese meals are stuffy and uncomfortable, but they really aren't! In fact, it's fun to take part in a real Japanese meal. It's almost like acting in a play.

Of all Japanese dishes I like Tempura best. First of all, I have a weakness for fried food. Second, you can put almost anything into a Tempura and it will taste great. I've cooked shrimp, eggplant, carrots, onions, tomatoes — even cheese. So add what you want to the recipe. And anything you don't like, don't cook.

The one thing you have to remember is to get everything ready before you begin cooking. Like most Japanese dishes, cooking Tempura takes only a minute or two. It's the preparation that is important. But it's worth it. You'll see!

When you eat, use the *waribashi* (chopsticks), not a fork. That makes the food taste even better, and the eating more fun.

Valerie Hayashida, 16

Fried Fish and Vegetables
Tempura

CAUTION!
THIS RECIPE CALLS FOR FRYING IN DEEP FAT.
DO NOT GO AHEAD UNTIL YOU READ PAGE 7.

Preparation and cooking time: about 1 hour　　　　　*Serves 4*

What You Need

BATTER
1 egg
½ cup of cold water
1 cup of all-purpose flour,
  sifted

DIPPING SAUCE
⅓ cup of mirin*
1 teaspoon of sugar
1 cup of chicken broth
⅓ cup of soy sauce
1 white radish or turnip,
  coarsely grated
freshly ground or pow-
  dered ginger

FISH AND VEGETABLES
12 sea scallops
12 shrimp, shelled and deveined
½ pound of white fish fillets, such as cod or haddock, cut into 2-inch
  squares

medium-sized mixing bowl
measuring cup
wire whisk or fork
flour sifter
long mixing spoon
measuring spoons
medium-sized saucepan
  with lid
grater
4 dipping bowls
2 small serving bowls
kitchen knife
cutting board
electric deep-fat fryer or
  wok
cooking thermometer
kitchen tongs, long-han-
  dled
paper towels
serving dish, heated

*A rice cooking wine; it is available in Oriental food stores and in many su-
permarkets.

8 fresh mushrooms
1 medium-sized onion,
   peeled and cut into ¼-
   inch slices
1 eggplant, cut into ½-inch
   slices
1 carrot, scraped and cut
   into ¼-inch slices
1 bamboo shoot, cut into
   very thin slices
4 cups of vegetable oil

What You Do

MAKE THE BATTER (STEPS 1–2)

1. Break the egg into the bowl, add the cold water, and beat thoroughly.
2. Gently stir in the flour until everything is well mixed. *Do not overstir.* Some lumps are okay.

MAKE THE DIPPING SAUCE (STEPS 3–6)

3. Mix the mirin and sugar.
4. Put the broth, mirin, and soy sauce in the saucepan.
5. Stir, bring the mixture to a boil over medium-high heat, then remove from the heat, cover, and keep warm.
6. When the tempura is ready, pour the dipping sauce into the dipping bowls, one for each person. Place the radish or turnip in one of the serving bowls and the ginger in the other.

COOK THE FISH AND VEGETABLES (STEPS 7–11)

7. Heat the oil in the fryer to 375°; if using a wok, heat the oil until it sizzles or the thermometer reads 375°.
8. Pat the fish and vegetables with paper towels *until they are thoroughly dry.*
9. Using the tongs, dip each piece of fish and vegetable into the batter, slide it gently into the hot oil, and cook until it is golden brown — about 1 minute on each side. Do not put all the ingredients into the batter at once; dip each piece separately, just before cooking. Be careful not to cook too many pieces at a time or the temperature of the oil will be lowered. Do not overcook — vegetables should be crisp, not soft.

10. Put the cooked food onto paper towels to drain; then, right away, transfer it to the heated serving dish and serve. Note that you don't fry all the food before serving it. You serve each batch immediately, so that it can be eaten while it is still hot and crisp.

11. The guests dip each piece of food into the dipping sauce before eating it. The Japanese would use chopsticks, but forks or fingers are okay too.

Lebanon

Since I am a "jr." in my family, I am better known as "Chip" to my friends. I am the youngest of three boys born and brought up in an American-Lebanese home. My grandparents migrated to the United States in the early 1900s, bringing with them their ethnic culture and cuisine. Both my parents inherited their Lebanese traditions from their parents and, in turn, shared them with my brothers and me.

I will always remember the delicious dishes my grandmother would prepare especially for us when she knew we were coming to visit. My mother inherited the same "special touch" from her mother for us to enjoy.

Among the dishes we especially like are stuffed grape leaves and stuffed zucchini, marinated lamb tongue, chick-pea dip, yogurt, and Lebanese bread. For dessert, we may have fresh fruit along with baklava, a delicious pastry prepared with a special dough, butter, walnuts, and syrup. No holiday is complete without "melt-in-your-mouth," delicate Lebanese pastries filled with dates and walnuts.

Sometimes our dishes may seem difficult to make. But to the Lebanese they are as simple to prepare as beef stew is for an American cook. The dishes I have included here are quite easy to make, however — and delicious to eat.

Raymond "Chip" Fadel, 18

Meat with Green Peas
Bazella be Laham

Preparation and cooking time: 1 ½ hours   *Serves 4*

What You Need

1 pound of beef or lamb,
cut into 1-inch cubes
2 tablespoons of butter or
margarine
1 large onion, chopped
dash of cinnamon
dash of allspice
½ teaspoon of salt
¼ teaspoon of pepper
1 small clove of garlic,
minced
½ cup of cold water
1 28-ounce can of tomatoes
2 16-ounce cans of peas,
drained; or 2 16-ounce
packages of frozen peas,
thawed

large pot with lid
measuring spoons
kitchen knife
cutting board
long mixing spoon
measuring cup

What You Do

1. Melt the butter or margarine in the pot over low heat. Add the meat and onions, raise the heat to medium, and cook until just brown.
2. Add the cinnamon, allspice, salt, pepper, and garlic. Turn down the heat to low, and cook the mixture, stirring constantly, until the onions are soft.
3. Add the water, cover the pot, and simmer about 30 minutes, or until the meat is tender (beef takes a bit longer). Add a little water if you need to as the meat simmers.
4. Add the tomatoes, with their juice, and bring the mixture to a boil.
5. Stir in the peas and lower the heat to keep the food warm. Serve over Rice Pilaf.

Rice Pilaf
Pilav

What You Need

2 tablespoons of butter or
  margarine
1 tablespoon of vermicelli
  broken into ½-inch
  pieces
1 cup of long-grain white
  rice, rinsed
1 teaspoon of salt
2 cups of boiling water

measuring spoons
large frying pan with lid
long mixing spoon
measuring cup
teakettle or saucepan

What You Do

1. Melt the butter or margarine over low heat in the frying pan. Add the vermicelli and cook over medium heat, stirring constantly until the pieces are lightly browned.
2. Add the rice and salt to the vermicelli. Stir to coat the rice with the butter.
3. Add the water and boil the mixture rapidly over high heat until ½ inch of water remains.
4. Turn the heat down to very low, cover the pan, and cook the rice for 20 minutes.
5. Turn off the heat and let the rice sit for a few minutes before serving.

Cucumber and Yogurt Salad

Preparation time: ½ hour   *Serves 4*

What You Need

1 small clove of garlic	kitchen knife
½ teaspoon of salt	cutting board
1 pint of plain yogurt	measuring spoons
1 large cucumber	garlic press (optional)
½ teaspoon of dried mint	large mixing bowl
leaves	long mixing spoon
fresh mint leaves (optional)	

What You Do

1. Slice the cucumber lengthwise in quarters, then in ¼-inch slices.
2. Put the salt and garlic clove in the mixing bowl and mash the garlic with the back of the spoon. (Or crush the garlic in a garlic press before putting it into the bowl.)
3. Add the yogurt, cucumber slices, and dried mint leaves. Mix thoroughly.
4. Serve the salad in individual bowls, garnished with fresh mint leaves if available.

Mexico

I have lived all my life in Los Angeles, California. I have four brothers and one sister. They were also born here in Los Angeles. My father came from El Paso, Texas, and my mother from Ensenada, Baja California. Some of my ancestors were native *norteamericanos,* while others came from Mexico.

My family and I enjoy eating both Mexican and American foods, just as we all enjoy speaking both Spanish and English. One of my favorite Mexican dishes is Bean Tostadas. Tostadas are very easy to make, and they are really delicious. Another good Mexican recipe is Guacamole, which is made from avocados. You can eat Guacamole as a salad on crisp lettuce, as a topping for tostadas, or as an appetizer with tortilla chips. If after eating a filling Mexican meal you have any room for dessert, try my recipe for Rice Pudding. I hope you like these recipes as much as I do. Good luck!

Gloria Nuñez, 18

Bean Tostadas
Tostadas de Frijoles

Preparation and cooking time: ½ hour, plus 1 hour for thawing the tortillas

Serves 2–3

What You Need

1 cup of canned refried beans*
1 tablespoon of cooking oil
6 frozen tortillas, thawed*
1 cup of shredded lettuce
1 large tomato, chopped
½ cup of shredded cheddar cheese
bottled hot pepper sauce (optional)

kitchen knife
cutting board
small saucepan
large frying pan
measuring spoons
spatula or pancake turner
paper towels

What You Do

1. Heat the beans over low heat in the saucepan for about 5 minutes, or until heated through.
2. Heat the oil in the frying pan over medium heat until it sizzles, and fry the tortillas for 1 minute on each side. Drain them on paper towels.
3. Spread some beans on each tortilla.
4. On top of the beans, sprinkle shredded lettuce and some tomato, and top with cheese. If you like spicy food, you may wish to put a few drops of hot pepper sauce on your tostada.

* These can be found in most supermarkets. Acceptable substitutes for the refried beans: chick peas, black beans, kidney beans, pinto beans.

Avocado Sauce
Guacamole

Preparation time: ½ hour *Serves 8*

What You Need

6 ripe avocados, peeled
  and pitted
2 teaspoons of lemon juice
2½ teaspoons of salt
1 small onion, finely
  chopped
1 small tomato, finely
  chopped
2 tablespoons of mayon-
  naise
1 teaspoon of salad oil
4 drops of Tabasco
lettuce or 1 package of tortilla chips

kitchen knife
cutting board
large mixing bowl
fork
measuring spoons
long mixing spoon

What You Do

1. Place the avocados in the bowl. Sprinkle them with the lemon juice and salt, and mash them with the fork.
2. Add the remaining ingredients and mix well. (If you are not serving the Guacamole right away, spread the mayonnaise on top to keep the mixture from darkening. Then do the mixing just before serving.)
3. Serve the Guacamole on crisp lettuce as a salad, or as an appetizer dip with tortilla chips.

Rice Pudding
Arroz con Leche

Preparation and cooking time: about 1¼ hours   *Serves 3–4*

What You Need

1½ cups of water
1 cup of rice (not instant)
1½ cups of sugar
½ teaspoon of cinnamon
½ cup of raisins
1 quart of fresh milk or 1
   large can of evaporated
   milk
whipped cream (optional;
   see "Whipping Cream,"
   p. 8)

measuring cup
medium-sized saucepan
   with lid
measuring spoons
long mixing spoon

What You Do

1. Bring the water to a boil over high heat, add the rice, turn the heat to low, and simmer the rice, covered, for about 40 minutes, or until nearly all the water has been absorbed.
2. Add the sugar, cinnamon, raisins, and milk. Mix thoroughly.
3. Cover the pan again and continue cooking for about 15 minutes over very low heat.
4. Remove the pan from the stove and let the pudding cool for about 10 minutes. Serve it warm or cold, with whipped cream if you wish.

Pakistan

I like to make all kinds of food, but Pakistani food is the kind I like to make best — probably because my mother is from Pakistan. After she married my father, they settled in Wilmette, Illinois, which is where we live now.

I have one sister who is a senior in college. My father is a professor of Asian studies and writes books on cultural history. Mother spends a lot of her time working for such organizations as the International Visitor's Center and the Hull House Association.

Mother usually cooks for our family. But when she is tired, busy, or just doesn't feel like cooking, we all pitch in.

Both of my recipes are from Pakistan. Tandoori is very similar to broiled chicken. The reason the chicken is called Tandoori is because originally it was cooked in a *tandoor,* which is an earthen oven that looks like a pot-bellied stove, only it's underground.

Badam Pista is a cross between toffee and fudge. I like to drink milk with it. It may be served as a dessert or as a snack.

Safia Welty, 13

Yogurt Chicken
Tandoori

Preparation and cooking time: about ¾ hour (the chicken must be refrigerated for an additional 4 hours)

What You Need

4 tablespoons of plain yogurt
½ cup of chopped green pepper
2 cloves of garlic, finely chopped
1 teaspoon of paprika
½ teaspoon of salt
chicken pieces (2 of each: legs, wings, thighs, breasts), skinned
butter or margarine
2 cups of white rice

kitchen knife
cutting board
large mixing bowl
measuring spoons
measuring cup
long mixing spoon
plastic wrap
shallow baking pan
kitchen tongs

What You Do

1. In the bowl, mix together the yogurt, green pepper, garlic, paprika, and salt.
2. Add the chicken pieces and stir until each piece is well coated. Cover the bowl with plastic wrap and refrigerate for 4 hours. (Or you can refrigerate it overnight if you like.)
3. Grease the baking pan with butter or margarine and place the coated chicken pieces in it in one layer.
4. Lower the broiler rack in the oven so that it is about 5 inches from the flame. Broil the chicken until it is brown on one side, about 10 minutes.
5. As soon as the chicken is in the broiler, begin preparing the rice according to the directions on the package. If you are using instant rice, you can wait until you have turned the chicken.
6. Turn the chicken pieces over and brown them on that side, about 10 minutes. Serve the chicken with the rice.

Coconut Almond Candy
Badam Pista

Preparation and cooking time: ¾ hour (candy must be refrigerated for an additional ¾ hour)

Makes 54 candies

What You Need

5 ounces of dry whole milk
½ cup of fresh milk
¾ cup of confectioners' sugar
1 tablespoon of butter or margarine
2 tablespoons of shredded coconut
2 tablespoons of chopped almonds
⅛ teaspoon of vanilla

measuring cup
medium-sized mixing bowl
long mixing spoon
measuring spoons
large saucepan
6- x 9-inch baking pan
kitchen knife

What You Do

1. Mix the dry milk and the fresh milk together in the bowl. Slowly add the sugar, stirring constantly.
2. Melt the butter or margarine in the saucepan over low heat. Add the mixture in the bowl to the melted butter in the pan. Turn up the heat to medium and cook for 5 minutes. Stir constantly, taking care not to let the mixture stick to the bottom of the pan.
3. Stir in the coconut, almonds, and vanilla. Cook for another 4 minutes, stirring constantly.
4. Remove the mixture from the heat. Spoon it into the baking pan and spread it evenly. Let it cool for 10 minutes. Then refrigerate it for 45 minutes.
5. After the candy has set, cut it into 1-inch squares and serve.

Philippines

"Aloha!" Although I was born in Minnesota, like my father, *aloha* was one of the first words I could speak. My mother was born in the Philippine Islands but reared on Kauai, the "garden island" of Hawaii. As a result, I am half black, half Filipino — and a little bit of Hawaiian too.

Because our family is so spread out, from Washington, D.C., where I live, to Minnesota, to Hawaii, our food is quite varied. But my favorites are Filipino dishes. Filipino food is a combination of Chinese, Spanish, Portuguese, and native island cooking. There is a lot of vinegar in Filipino cooking, and the main dishes are almost always served over, or with, rice.

Two dishes I'd like to share are Chicken Adobo, the national dish of the Philippines, and Meatballs and Mochi Rice, which requires a special kind of rice that is sweet and sticky. I hope you enjoy them.

Derek Peake, 16

Chicken Adobo
Adobong Mankok

What You Need

1 3-pound frying chicken, cut into serving pieces	kitchen knife
1 teaspoon of salt	cutting board
¼ teaspoon of pepper	measuring spoons
½ cup of vinegar	large frying pan with lid
2 cups of cold water	measuring cup
2 tablespoons of soy sauce	kitchen tongs
1 clove of garlic, minced	
1 bay leaf	
2 tablespoons of cooking oil	

What You Do

1. Sprinkle salt and pepper on the chicken pieces. Let them stand for about 15 minutes.
2. Put them in the frying pan. Add the vinegar, water, soy sauce, garlic, and bay leaf.
3. Bring to a boil over high heat, reduce the heat to low, cover the pan, and simmer gently for about 30 minutes, or until the liquid has almost evaporated.
4. Add the cooking oil and fry the chicken pieces uncovered over high heat. Turn the pieces with the tongs until they are brown on all sides. Serve hot.

Meatballs and Mochi Rice

Preparation and cooking time: about 1½ hours (the mochi rice must soak for an additional hour)

Serves 3–4

What You Need

¾ cup of mochi rice* or
  white rice (not instant)
4 tablespoons of soy sauce
2 tablespoons of cornstarch
2 tablespoons of sherry
3 tablespoons of oil
1 pound of ground beef
4 tablespoons of hot water

measuring cup
sieve
measuring spoons
large mixing bowl
long mixing spoon
plate
oven-proof dish
large pot with lid
small bowl

What You Do

1. Rinse the mochi rice in the sieve under cold water. Then soak it in a bowl with 2 cups of cold water for at least 1 hour. Then drain the water off. (Omit this step if you are using white rice.)
2. In the mixing bowl, combine the cornstarch, sherry, oil, and 3 tablespoons of the soy sauce. Mix in the ground beef.
3. Form the beef mixture into meatballs about 2 inches in diameter. Spread the rice on a plate. Roll the meatballs in the rice, coating them thoroughly.
4. Put the coated meatballs in one layer in the oven-proof dish and set it into a big pot that has at least 1½ inches of water in it. Cover the pot, bring the water to a boil over high heat, lower the heat to medium, and steam for 35 minutes.
5. In the small bowl, mix the remaining tablespoon of soy sauce with the hot water. Pour the mixture over the meatballs and steam for 30 minutes longer. Serve immediately.

* This can be found in an Oriental market.

Poland

I am a senior in high school in Morrisville, Pennsylvania, and am third-generation Polish. I hope to go to college and major in nursing, but my hobby is cooking.

I guess liking to cook runs in my family. My older sister Donna is a dietitian, and my mother is a store manager for a gourmet food shop. She is also a gourmet cook. My grandmother, who left Poland with my grandfather to find better opportunities in the United States, was noted for her Polish recipes. Polish food for the most part is very bland. That is why my grandmother's cooking was so special. Hers always had spices.

As a child I used to look forward to visiting my grandparents on a Saturday, when my grandmother prepared a dinner of Green Bean Soup, Tasty Pork, parsley potatoes, and Dilled Cucumber Salad. She usually made Poppy Seed Cake for dessert. After dinner the adults would play pinochle and finish up all the leftovers.

On Sundays Polish people always eat chicken soup and stewed chicken. On holidays we have dishes like sautéed mushrooms in sour-cream sauce, sauerkraut soup, and pierogis, which are delicious meat-filled turnovers.

Because of my childhood memories, I particularly like to prepare my grandmother's special Saturday menu.

Maureen Cader, 17

Green Bean Soup
Zupa Fasola

Preparation and cooking time: 1¾ hours   *Serves 4–6*

What You Need

1 pound of fresh or frozen
  green beans, cut into
  small pieces
water
1 ham bone or smoked
  hock
3 tablespoons of white vinegar
¼ teaspoon of sugar
4 strips of bacon
1 tablespoon of flour
¼ cup of milk

kitchen knife
cutting board
large pot with lid
measuring spoons
large frying pan
long mixing spoon
measuring cup

What You Do

1. Place the beans in a large pot and add enough water to cover them. Add the ham bone or smoked hock and bring the water to a boil over high heat. Turn the heat to low and simmer the soup, covered, until the beans are tender.
2. Stir in the vinegar and sugar. Put the lid back on and remove the pot from the heat.
3. In the frying pan, fry the bacon until it is crisp. Remove the bacon and reserve it.
4. Over low heat, stir the flour into the bacon fat in the pan. Gradually add the milk, stirring constantly, to make a thick paste.
5. Blend the fat mixture into the soup, reheat, and serve it immediately, garnished with crumbled bacon.

Tasty Pork
Smaczna Wieprzawina

Preparation and roasting time: 2½–3 hours (in addition, the meat must be refrigerated for 24 hours)   *Serves 4–6*

What You Need

4- to 5-pound fresh pork
shoulder
1 tablespoon of pickling
spice, with cloves and
cinnamon sticks re-
moved
2 cloves of garlic, minced
1 teaspoon of salt
½ teaspoon of pepper

small mixing bowl
measuring spoons
kitchen knife
cutting board
waxed paper
baking pan

What You Do

1. In the bowl mix together the pickling spice, garlic, salt, and pepper.
2. Rub the seasoning well over the meaty side (not the fatty side) of the pork. Cover the meat with waxed paper and refrigerate it for at least 24 hours.
3. Preheat the oven to 450°.
4. Place the pork in the baking pan with the fat side up and bake for 15 minutes.
5. Reduce the heat to 350°. Cook the meat until it is done (allow 30 to 35 minutes to the pound). If you are using a meat thermometer, it should register well-done.

Dilled Cucumber Salad

Preparation time: 30 minutes (cucumbers must stand at room temperature for an additional 30 minutes)   *Serves 6*

What You Need

3 medium-sized cucumbers
1¼ teaspoons of salt
¼ teaspoon of pepper
2 tablespoons of sugar
2 tablespoons of white vinegar
3 tablespoons of water
1 tablespoon of fresh dill, minced, or 1 teaspoon of dried dill weed

kitchen knife
cutting board
measuring spoons
large mixing bowl
saucer or small plate
strainer or colander
small mixing bowl
long kitchen spoon
salad fork and spoon

What You Do

1. Thinly slice the cucumbers and place them in the large bowl. Sprinkle them with ¼ teaspoon of the salt.
2. Weigh down the cucumbers with the saucer or small plate. Let them stand at room temperature for 30 minutes.
3. Drain the cucumbers thoroughly.
4. In the small bowl, combine the rest of the ingredients and mix well.
5. Pour this mixture over the drained cucumbers and toss with the salad fork and spoon. Chill the salad before serving.

Poppy Seed Cake
Tort Makowy

Preparation and baking time: about 2 hours (includes cooling the cake)

Serves 8–10

What You Need

1 cup (2 sticks) of butter or margarine, at room temperature
1½ cups of sugar
4 eggs
1 teaspoon of vanilla
1 jar of poppy seed filling
1 cup of chopped walnuts
2 cups of flour
1 teaspoon of baking soda
½ teaspoon of salt
1 cup of sour cream
confectioners' sugar

2 small bowls
measuring cup
wooden spoon
large mixing bowl
measuring spoons
kitchen knife
medium-sized mixing bowl
egg beater
10-inch tube pan
wire rack

What You Do

1. Preheat the oven to 350°.
2. Separate the eggs (see the instructions on p. 7).
3. Cream the butter or margarine in the large bowl. Add the sugar and beat the mixture well. Add the egg yolks and beat them thoroughly into the mixture. Stir in the vanilla, poppy seed filling, and nuts.
4. In the medium-sized bowl, combine the flour, baking soda, and salt, and stir the mixture into the batter. Stir in the sour cream.
5. In the small bowl, beat the egg whites until they are stiff and fold the whites into the cake mixture.
6. Grease and lightly flour the tube pan. Pour in the batter and bake the cake for 1 hour.
7. Remove it from the oven and let it cool for 10 minutes. Take it out of the pan and place it on the wire rack. When the cake has completely cooled, sprinkle it with confectioners' sugar.

Polynesia

I have lived in Honolulu, Hawaii, for most of my life, except for the four years I spent as a student in San Francisco and Boston. My grandparents were originally from China and immigrated to Hawaii in the early 1900s. According to my parents, both of my grandmothers were "picture" brides, but this wasn't a factor in determining the size of their families — my father had nine brothers and sisters, and my mother, eleven! Big families are an important part of the Chinese culture, and if you consider having five sons a large family, then my parents have held on to the tradition.

Growing up in Hawaii was quite a cultural experience because there are so many different races, each with its own ways. The people of Hawaii have assimilated a variety of eating customs, and this makes dinner in Hawaiian homes truly cosmopolitan. Dinner in our home one evening may consist of Japanese or Chinese food, the next night it may be a Hawaiian luau, and the following night we may find steak and potatoes on the table.

My favorite food is Chinese. Chinese meals usually have rice, a vegetable dish mixed with meat, and a seafood dish. The vegetable dish usually consists of chopped vegetables and slices of meat. The reason for this is that the Chinese believe that carving should be done in the kitchen and that guests should not be asked to cut their meat at the table. In cooking, the vegetables must be cut into small pieces and cooked quickly to preserve their color and flavor. This custom was probably originally caused by the lack of fuel in China.

Stuart Pang, 19

Fried Rice
Chao Fan

Preparation and cooking time: ½ hour   *Serves 6*

What You Need

3 cups of white rice
3 tablespoons of salad or
    peanut oil
½ cup of diced cooked
    chicken
½ cup of diced cooked
    ham
2 dried mushrooms, soaked
    and chopped,* or 2 fresh
    mushrooms, chopped
½ teaspoon of salt
2 tablespoons of soy sauce
2 tablespoons of oyster
    sauce or soy sauce†
½ cup of fresh peas or fro-
    zen peas, thawed
½ cup of chopped green
    onion
3 eggs, beaten

measuring cup
medium-sized saucepan
    with lid
kitchen knife
cutting board
measuring spoons
large frying pan
small mixing bowl
egg beater or wire whisk
spatula

What You Do

1. Cook the rice according to the directions on the package.
2. Heat the oil in the frying pan until it sizzles. Add the chicken, ham, and mushrooms, and stir-fry over high heat for 2 minutes.
3. Add the salt, soy sauce, and oyster sauce. Continue cooking for 1 minute, stirring.
4. Stir in the rice, peas, onions, and eggs. Cook for 2 minutes, stirring to break up the eggs. Serve at once.

* If using dried mushrooms, put them in a bowl, pour boiling water over them to cover, and let them stand for 15 minutes. Drain them and squeeze out the excess water. Then chop them.
† Oyster sauce can be found, bottled, in many supermarkets and in any Oriental market.

Beef and Tomatoes
Niu Ro Tsao Fan Chieh

Preparation and cooking time: about 1 hour   *Serves 4*

What You Need

1 pound of beef round or
   flank steak, sliced into
   strips ⅛-inch thick
4 tablespoons of peanut oil
1 teaspoon of soy sauce
2 teaspoons of flour
1 clove of garlic
2 medium onions, cut into
   large pieces
1 green pepper, cut into
   large pieces
3 medium-sized tomatoes,
   cut into wedges

kitchen knife
cutting board
medium-sized mixing bowl
small mixing bowl
measuring spoons
large frying pan
long mixing spoon

What You Do

1. Place the meat slices in the larger mixing bowl. In the small bowl mix together 1 tablespoon of the oil, the soy sauce, and the flour. Pour the gravy over the meat strips and let the mixture stand for 10–15 minutes.
2. Heat 2 tablespoons of the oil in the frying pan and add the garlic. Press the garlic clove against the sides of the pan. When it is brown and dry, remove it.
3. Add the meat and gravy to the pan and cook the mixture over medium-high heat for about 5 minutes, stirring frequently. Remove the meat and set it aside.
4. To the gravy in the pan, add the remaining oil (1 tablespoon), onion, and green pepper. Cook over medium-high heat for 3 minutes, stirring frequently.
5. Add the meat and tomatoes to the pan. Stir the mixture gently and heat it until the gravy begins to bubble. (Do not overcook. Overcooking toughens the meat and makes the tomatoes mushy.) Serve at once.

Pineapple Shrimp

Preparation and cooking time: 1¼ hours   *Serves 6*

What You Need

1 pound of fresh shrimp, shelled and deveined
1 egg, slightly beaten
½ cup of cracker crumbs
½ cup of flour
1½ teaspoons of salt
2 cups of oil
sugar
1 tablespoon of vinegar
½ cup of water
¼ red chili pepper, chopped, or ¼ teaspoon of crushed dry red pepper
1 small, fresh pineapple, cubed, or 1 8-ounce can of pineapple chunks, drained
1 tablespoon of cornstarch
1 tablespoon of water

kitchen knife
cutting board
medium-sized mixing bowl
small mixing bowl
fork or wire whisk
plate
measuring cup
measuring spoons
serving platter
electric deep-fat fryer
paper towels
small saucepan
long mixing spoon

What You Do

1. Cut each shrimp in half lengthwise and place the halves in the larger bowl. Add the egg, mix well, and let the mixture stand for 15 minutes.
2. Combine the cracker crumbs, flour, and 1 teaspoon of the salt on the plate. Roll each shrimp in this mixture. Place the serving platter in the oven and turn the thermostat to 300°.

3. Heat the oil in the fryer until it reaches the temperature recommended by the manufacturer. Fry the shrimp in the hot oil, a few at a time, until they are golden brown. Remove them from the oil, drain them on paper towels, place them on the heated serving platter, and set it aside.
4. In the saucepan combine the remaining ½ teaspoon of salt, the vinegar, water, and chili pepper. Add sugar to taste. Add the pineapple and cook the mixture for 10 minutes over low heat.
5. In the measuring cup mix the cornstarch and the tablespoon of water together until smooth and add to the saucepan. Bring the mixture to a boil over medium heat, stirring constantly. Pour over the shrimp and serve.

Portugal

My father brought me to Bristol, Rhode Island, from the Azores when I was just a baby. My mother had died and my father did not want to stay there anymore. He had many friends in Bristol.

The Azores are islands in the Atlantic Ocean about seven hundred miles west of Portugal, the country that owns them. I have never been there, but I want to go someday.

My father's father and his people were whalers. In fact, some Azoreans still hunt whales the way it was done a hundred years ago, with hand harpoons. Whalers from Nantucket and New Bedford taught the Azoreans how to hunt whales that way.

My father is not a fisher. He doesn't even like to get on any kind of boat! He is a schoolteacher and a musician. He likes to cook and eat Portuguese food. And he is giving me cooking lessons.

Eggs and Onions Coimbra is our favorite breakfast. Coimbra is the name of the place where my father went to college. I like Noodles and Tuna because it is easy to make. I hope you like these recipes, too.

Robert Da Sousa, 14

Eggs and Onions Coimbra

Preparation and cooking time: ½ hour   *Serves 4*

What You Need

2 tablespoons of butter or
  margarine
4 small onions, thinly sliced
¼ cup of plain croutons
8 eggs
½ teaspoon of salt
¼ teaspoon of black pepper
paprika

large frying pan
kitchen knife
cutting board
spatula or slotted spoon
measuring cup
paper towels
medium-sized bowl
measuring spoons
fork or wire whisk
serving platter, heated

What You Do

1. Melt the butter or margarine over low heat in the frying pan. Add the sliced onions and cook until light brown.
2. Add the croutons. Cook them 2–3 minutes, turning constantly with the spatula, until all sides are golden.
3. Take the croutons out of the pan and drain them on a paper towel.
4. Break the eggs into the bowl, add the salt and pepper, and beat them thoroughly. Add them to the onions in the pan and cook the mixture until the eggs are firm (about 3 minutes), stirring constantly.
5. Put the eggs on the serving platter, sprinkle them with paprika, and top with croutons. Serve immediately.

Noodles and Tuna

Preparation and cooking time: 1½ hours   *Serves 4–6*

What You Need

1 tablespoon of cooking oil
1 clove of garlic, sealed
½ pound of fresh mush-
  rooms, thinly sliced
1 cup of tomato sauce
1 cup of cold water
1 teaspoon of salt
¼ teaspoon of pepper
¼ teaspoon of basil
1 pound of noodles
1 7-ounce can of tuna,
  packed in water
1 tablespoon of dried parsley flakes

kitchen knife
cutting board
measuring spoons
large frying pan with lid
measuring cup
long mixing spoon
large pot with lid
fork
colander

What You Do

1. Heat the oil over low heat in the frying pan.
2. Add the garlic and mushrooms. Cook about 4 minutes, until the garlic is golden brown. Then remove the garlic.
3. Add the tomato sauce, water, salt, pepper, and basil to the pan. Mix well. Cover and cook, still over low heat, for 45 minutes.
4. About 15 minutes before the sauce is done, put on the water for the noodles and cook them according to the directions on the package.
5. While the noodles are cooking, drain the tuna and break it up with a fork. When Step 3 is completed, add the tuna and the parsley flakes to the sauce, mix thoroughly, and cook 10 minutes more.
6. When the noodles are done, drain them in the colander and serve the tuna mixture over them.

Puerto Rico

Our family came from Puerto Rico in 1964. I have two younger sisters, Lissette and Maritza.

I learned to cook when I was about nine years old by watching my mother and my grandmother. I enjoy cooking very much. Since my mother and father both have to work late, my sister Lissette and I fix supper. When they come home, dinner is all ready to be served. My mother is very happy with us because we help her a lot.

I like to cook both American and Puerto Rican dishes. One of my favorite American meals is pork chops with mashed potatoes.

Because of Puerto Rico's sunny tropical climate, there are many fresh fruits, such as oranges, lemons, and bananas. These tropical fruits are used for many Puerto Rican drinks and desserts. Two fruit recipes I like to make are Banana Cake and Orange Pudding.

Arline Ortiz, 13

Banana Cake
Torta Plátanos

Preparation and baking time: 1 ¾ hours   *Serves 8*

What You Need

1 stick (½ cup) of butter or
   margarine, at room temperature
½ cup of sugar
1 egg
2 cups plus 1 teaspoon of
   flour
1 tablespoon of baking
   powder
½ teaspoon of salt
½ teaspoon of nutmeg
2 large, ripe bananas
1 teaspoon of vanilla
½ cup of raisins
½ cup of coarsely chopped
   pecans

2 large mixing bowls
large wooden spoon
flour sifter
measuring cup
measuring spoons
2 small mixing bowls
9 x 5 x 3-inch loaf pan

What You Do

1. Preheat the oven to 350°.
2. In one of the large bowls cream together the butter and sugar with the wooden spoon until the mixture is light and fluffy. Add the egg and beat the mixture thoroughly.
3. Into the other large bowl sift together 2 cups of flour and the baking powder, salt, and nutmeg.
4. In one of the small bowls, mash the bananas, add the vanilla, and mix thoroughly.
5. Add the banana-vanilla mixture to the butter mixture alternately with the dry ingredients, beating after each addition until the batter is thoroughly blended.
6. In the other small bowl, mix the raisins, the remaining teaspoon of flour, and the pecans together. Stir them into the batter and mix well.

7. Grease the loaf pan with a little butter or margarine and pour in the batter. Bake the bread for 1 hour. Cool and serve warm or chilled.

Orange Pudding
Pudín de Naranja

Preparation and baking time: 1¼ hours   *Serves 4*

What You Need

1¼ cups plus 1 teaspoon of
  sugar
6 eggs
juice of 2 oranges
rind of 2 oranges, grated
1 tablespoon of butter or
  margarine, at room tem-
  perature
whipped cream (see
  "Whipping Cream,"
  p. 8)

2 medium-sized mixing
  bowls
measuring cup
grater
fruit juicer
egg beater
wooden spoon
2-quart casserole
kitchen knife
serving dish

What You Do

1. Preheat the oven to 350°.
2. In one of the bowls, beat 1¼ cups of the sugar, the eggs, orange juice, and rind together.
3. In the other bowl, cream together the butter and the remaining teaspoon of sugar until the mixture is very soft. Add this to the first mixture and mix thoroughly.
4. Grease the casserole with butter or margarine. Pour in the pudding mixture and bake for 45 minutes. Cool and chill.
5. Unmold the pudding onto a serving dish. To unmold, run a knife around the edges to loosen. Place the serving dish over the casserole and, holding the dish in place, quickly turn the casserole upside down. Lift the casserole away from the dish. Garnish the pudding with whipped cream and serve.

Sicily

I am a high school student at Sacred Heart Academy in Stamford, Connecticut. Although cooking may not be my first love, I can surely say that eating good food is.

My father came from a small town in Sicily called Campofelice, which in English means "field of happiness." Campofelice is right on the outskirts of Cefalie, a famous seaside resort.

This past summer I visited Sicily for the first time. It was my father's first visit back in seventeen years! Needless to say, it was a memorable experience. It was on this fantastic trip that I learned about and tasted many of the varied and delicious Sicilian dishes. Sicilian food is quite different from the kind of Italian food my mother always cooked, since her parents came from a different part of Italy. Here are some of my favorite Sicilian dishes, which I now help my mother cook at home.

Marianne Rizzo, 16

Sicilian Tomato Salad
Insalata Siciliana

Preparation time: ½ hour *Serves 6*

What You Need

6 large, ripe tomatoes
½ teaspoon of salt
4 ounces of mushrooms,
    bottled in oil, drained
4 ounces of Italian-style
    pickles, drained
25 pitted black olives
4 teaspoons of capers
2½ tablespoons of cooked
    peas
1 cup of mayonnaise
salt and pepper

kitchen knife
cutting board
small spoon
large mixing bowl
measuring spoons
measuring cup
wooden spoon
serving dish

What You Do

1. Rinse the tomatoes and cut off their tops. Scoop out the seeds and pulp carefully with the small spoon and discard them. Sprinkle the insides with salt. Turn the tomatoes upside down to drain.
2. Coarsely chop the mushrooms, pickles, and olives. Put them in the bowl with the capers and peas. Add the mayonnaise, sprinkle lightly with salt and pepper, and mix with the wooden spoon.
3. Sprinkle the insides of the drained tomatoes with pepper and fill them with the mixture. If any is left over, place it in a mound on the serving dish and surround it with the stuffed tomatoes.

Sicilian Beefsteak
Bistecche alla Siciliana

Preparation and cooking time: about ¾ hour   *Serves 6*

What You Need

6 large, ripe tomatoes
½ cup of olive oil
2 cloves of garlic
6 small beefsteaks, ¼ to ½
   pound each
½ cup of small, pickled
   sweet peppers, sliced
½ stalk of celery, diced
½ cup of pitted black
   olives
2 or 3 tablespoons of
   capers
salt and pepper
1 teaspoon of oregano

paring knife
cutting board
garlic press or heavy knife
measuring cup
large frying pan
spatula
cutting board
measuring spoons

What You Do

1. Skin the tomatoes (see the instructions on p. 8). Chop them into small pieces, discarding the seeds.
2. Crush the garlic, either in a garlic press or with a heavy knife.
3. Heat the olive oil in the frying pan over medium heat and sauté the garlic until it is brown. Discard the garlic.
4. In the same pan, sear the steaks over high heat for 2 minutes on each side.
5. Add the tomatoes, peppers, celery, olives, and capers to the pan. Season with salt and pepper to taste. Add the oregano.
6. Cook the mixture over medium heat until the meat is done to your taste, and serve the beefsteaks covered with the sauce.

Apple Fritters
Frittedde di Mela

Preparation and cooking time: about 1½ hours (apples must stand for an additional hour)

Makes 2 dozen

What You Need

6 tart apples
2 tablespoons of lemon juice
2 tablespoons of sugar
1 teaspoon of cinnamon
2 eggs
¼ cup of milk
1 teaspoon of oil
pinch of salt
2 teaspoons of baking powder
1 cup of flour
oil for frying
granulated sugar

vegetable peeler
kitchen knife
cutting board
measuring spoons
3 medium-sized mixing bowls
egg beater or wire whisk
large mixing bowl
measuring cup
flour sifter
long mixing spoon
electric deep-fat fryer
long-handled tongs
slotted spoon
paper towels

What You Do

1. Core, peel, and slice the apples into ¼-inch slices. Put the slices in one of the medium-sized bowls, sprinkle them with the lemon juice, sugar, and cinnamon, and let them stand for 1 hour.
2. Separate the eggs (see the instructions on p. 7), putting the whites into one of the medium-sized bowls and the yolks into the other.

3. Beat the egg yolks until they are thick and lemon-colored. Add the milk and the oil, and mix well.
4. Sift the salt, baking powder, and flour together into the large bowl. Add the yolk mixture and beat with the mixing spoon until the batter is smooth.
5. Beat the egg whites until they are stiff and fold them into the batter.
6. Pour 2 inches of oil into the fryer and heat it to the temperature recommended by the manufacturer for fritters. Dip the apple slices in the batter with the tongs and fry them in the hot oil until they are brown and puffy (about 3 minutes). Remove them with the slotted spoon, drain them on paper towels, and sprinkle them with granulated sugar. Serve immediately.

South Africa

My family moved from Capetown, South Africa, six years ago because of my father's job. We spent two years in Paris, France, before moving to the United States.

The pace here is much faster than in South Africa. Americans also watch a lot more television. TV came to South Africa only a short time ago, and it is aired just two hours a day, one hour in English and one hour in Afrikaans, which is a mixture of Dutch, German, and English. English and Afrikaans are the two official languages of South Africa.

I live with my family in Old Greenwich, Connecticut. I like living here, but I'm sometimes homesick for South Africa. Two of the things I miss most are the weather (South Africa has clear air and warm, sunny days all year round — we even went to the beach at Christmas!) and the wonderful food. Whenever I think of home, I like to make Tomatoe Bredie and Melk Tart, which are my favorites. Tomatoe Bredie is like a lamb stew and is just great for parties. Melk Tart (*melk* is Afrikaans for "milk") is like a milk custard with cinnamon. As far as I know, it is exclusively a Capetown recipe.

Susan Barlow, 18

Lamb Stew
Tomatoe Bredie

Preparation and cooking time: about 3 hours　　　　　*Serves 4–6*

What You Need

3 tablespoons of butter or margarine

2 medium-sized onions, sliced

1½–2 pounds of lamb, cut into 1-inch cubes

6–8 large, ripe tomatoes, sliced

2 teaspoons of sugar

1 teaspoon of salt

1¼ teaspoons of pepper

4–6 cups of rice

kitchen knife

cutting board

measuring spoons

large frying pan with lid

spatula

long mixing spoon

measuring cup

large saucepan with lid

What You Do

1. Melt the butter or margarine in the frying pan. Add the onions and fry them until they are lightly browned.
2. Add the lamb cubes and fry them quickly over high heat, turning them so they brown on all sides. Pour off most of the fat into an empty can and turn down the heat to low.
3. Add the tomatoes, sugar, salt, and pepper to the lamb and onion mixture and mix well.
4. Cover the pan tightly and simmer for 2–2½ hours, or until the lamb is tender.
5. About half an hour before the stew is done, begin preparing the rice according to the directions on the package. If you are using instant rice, make the rice just before the stew is done. Serve the stew over the rice.

Milk Tart
Melk Tart

Preparation and baking time: 1½ hours   *Serves 8*

What You Need

2 cups of milk	medium-sized saucepan
1 stick of cinnamon	measuring cup
1 tablespoon of flour	medium-sized mixing bowl
1 tablespoon of cornstarch	measuring spoons
4 tablespoons of sugar	wooden spoon
½ teaspoon of salt	small mixing bowl
½ tablespoon of butter or margarine	egg beater
2 eggs	
1 prebaked pie shell*	
cinnamon sugar	

What You Do

1. Put the milk and cinnamon stick in the saucepan and bring the milk to a boil. Remove the cinnamon stick and turn off the heat.
2. In the medium-sized bowl, combine the flour, cornstarch, sugar, and salt. Gradually add the milk, stirring with the wooden spoon.
3. Pour the mixture back into the saucepan and bring it to a boil, stirring constantly. Turn down the heat to low and simmer, still stirring constantly, until the mixture thickens. Remove the saucepan from the heat, stir in the butter or margarine, and allow the mixture to cool.
4. Preheat the oven to 425°.
5. Break the eggs into the small bowl and beat them until they are fluffy. Add them to the thickened milk mixture and pour it into the prebaked pie shell.

* You can buy frozen, unbaked pie shells in the supermarket. Bake according to the directions on the package.

6. Bake the tart for 10 minutes. Lower the temperature to 350°
   and continue baking for another 10 minutes, or until the tart
   has risen. Remove from the oven and sprinkle cinnamon sugar
   on top. Cool before serving.

Sweden

My mother immigrated to the United States from Gamelgaard, Sweden, in the 1940s, not speaking a word of English. She came here to marry my father, who had arrived two years before from Oslo, Norway. They wanted to raise a family in America.

Our whole family (six children) loves my mother's Swedish cooking, which is very rich and tasty. Since both of my parents work, my brothers and sister and I often cook dinner, using my mother's recipes.

Swedish people love to eat. They usually have one big meal a day, generally around noontime. The meals feature some type of soup (to warm you up on a cold winter day); an entree, usually a meat or seafood dish; a lot of cooked vegetables, such as squash; and, of course, some Scandinavian cheese from a nearby dairy farm.

Because of the big, rich meals, desserts are not usually sweet as they are in this country. Fruit and cheese is a customary dessert. Pastry or crêpes are common also.

Here are some of my family's favorite Swedish dishes.

Jayne Seebold, 19

Sailor's Beef
Sjömansbiff

Preparation and cooking time: about 2½ hours   *Serves 3-4*

What You Need

6 medium-sized potatoes
3 onions
2 tablespoons of butter or
   margarine
1 pound of beef chuck or 1
   pound of ground beef
1 teaspoon of salt
black pepper
2 cups of water or beef
   bouillon
a few sprigs of parsley,
   chopped

potato peeler
kitchen knife
cutting board
large frying pan
long kitchen spoon
2-quart, stove-top casserole
   with lid

What You Do

1. Peel the potatoes and cut them into pieces ½-inch thick. Peel and cut the onions into wedges. Trim any excess fat off the chuck and cut it into bite-sized pieces.
2. Heat the butter or margarine in the frying pan over medium heat and sauté the onions until they are soft, stirring occasionally.
3. Add the meat to the pan, mix it into the onions, and cook, stirring occasionally, until the meat is browned.
4. In the casserole, put a layer of the meat mixture and then a layer of potatoes. Sprinkle each layer with salt and pepper, and continue layering until all the potatoes are used. A layer of potatoes should be on top.
5. Pour enough water or bouillon over the casserole to barely cover the potatoes and bring to a boil over high heat. Turn the heat to low and simmer the casserole, covered, for 1 to 1½ hours or until the meat is tender and the potatoes are cooked through. Sprinkle the dish with the chopped parsley and serve.

Pea Soup with Pork
Ärter med Fläsk

Preparation and cooking time: 1½–2 hours (the peas must soak for an additional hour)   *Serves 6–8*

What You Need

1 pound (2 cups) of dried yellow split peas
5 cups of water
3 medium-sized onions
½ to 1 pound of lean salt pork
2 whole cloves
1 teaspoon of marjoram
½ teaspoon of thyme
salt and pepper

large pot with lid
measuring cup
kitchen knife
cutting board
long mixing spoon

What You Do

1. Rinse the peas. Put them in the pot with the water and bring to a boil over high heat. Boil for 2–3 minutes. Then turn off the heat and let the peas soak for 1 hour. Skim the residue from the top.
2. Peel one onion and stud it with the cloves. Peel the others and chop them finely.
3. Add the pork, onions, marjoram, and thyme to the peas.
4. Turn the heat to low and simmer the soup, partially covered, for 1–1½ hours, or until the peas are tender.
5. Remove the whole onion and the pork. Cut the pork into bite-sized pieces and return it to the soup. Add salt and pepper to taste and serve piping hot.

Swedish Pancake Torte
Plättartårta

Preparation and baking time: about 1 hour   *Serves 8–10*

What You Need

16 ounces of applesauce
½ cup of firmly packed
  brown sugar
¼ teaspoon of cinnamon
1 cup of *sifted* flour (see
  p. 4)
1 teaspoon of baking pow-
  der
3 eggs
1 cup of granulated sugar
½ cup of melted butter or
  margarine
whipped cream (see
  "Whipping Cream,"
  p. 8)

measuring cup
measuring spoons
medium-sized saucepan
long mixing spoon
flour sifter
medium-sized mixing bowl
large mixing bowl
electric mixer or egg
  beater
4 pie plates (8- or 9-inch)
spatula
platter
round serving plate

What You Do

1. In the saucepan stir together the applesauce, brown sugar, and cinnamon. Bring the mixture to a boil over medium heat. Turn the heat to low and simmer, stirring often, for 10–12 minutes, or until the mixture is smooth. Let it cool in the pan while you do the baking.

2. Preheat the oven to 425°.

3. Sift together the flour and baking powder into the smaller bowl.

4. Break the eggs into the large bowl, add the granulated sugar, and beat with an electric mixer or egg beater until the mixture thickens. Fold in the flour mixture with the mixing spoon and add the melted butter.

5. Pour the batter evenly into the 4 pie plates. Bake the pancakes until the batter is light brown (about 5 minutes). Remove the pancakes with a spatula and set them on a platter to cool. Cool for about 15 minutes.

6. Spread the applesauce mixture over three of the pancakes and stack them on the serving plate, one on top of the other. Place the fourth pancake on top. Spread it with whipped cream and serve.

United States
New England

My grandmother's maternal grandfather was a whaling captain out of New Bedford, Massachusetts. Her father was a native American. So you can see that my roots in New England go way back.

Then what am I doing in California? My mother is a book editor, and she is working on some history books here. I like California people and the weather. But I'll be glad to get back to New England!

New England cooking uses all the things that grow or can be caught in the area, many of them from the sea. New Englanders eat lots of fish and shellfish, such as clams, oysters, and scallops.

Two of my favorite dishes are Clam Chowder and Maple Pumpkin Pie, which combines the great tastes of maple syrup and pumpkin. Hot Mulled Cider is a warming drink on a cold winter evening.

I started cooking when I was about six years old. I've taken lessons and learned a lot. Now I cook all the time. I like cooking. It's fun to create something and then have people say, "That's wonderful!"

Jesse Lynch, 14

Hot Mulled Cider

Preparation and cooking time: ½ hour   *Serves 8*

What You Need

2 quarts of apple cider
¾ cup of brown sugar
11 sticks of cinnamon (8 optional) ·
1 teaspoon of whole cloves
1 teaspoon of allspice

large saucepan
measuring cup
measuring spoons
cheesecloth
scissors
string

What You Do

1. Pour the cider into the saucepan. Add the brown sugar.
2. Tie the cloves, allspice, and 3 of the cinnamon sticks in a square of cheesecloth. Put this into the cider.
3. Bring the cider to a boil over medium heat. Turn the heat to low and simmer for 10 minutes.
4. Remove the bag of spices and serve the cider hot in individual cups. You may want to put one cinnamon stick into each cup before you pour in the cider.

New England Clam Chowder

Preparation and cooking time: 1½ hours   *Serves 6–8*

What You Need

2 ounces of salt pork, diced
1 medium onion, chopped
8 6½-ounce cans of chopped
  clams
2 medium-sized potatoes,
  peeled and diced
2 cups of evaporated milk
2 tablespoons of butter or
  margarine
salt and pepper
oyster crackers (optional)

kitchen knife
cutting board
vegetable peeler
large frying pan
slotted spoon
medium-sized bowl
measuring cup
measuring spoons
large saucepan
long mixing spoon

What You Do

1. Fry the salt pork in the frying pan over medium heat until brown. Remove the pork with the slotted spoon and discard.
2. Add the onions to the pan and cook them until they are soft (about 3 minutes).
3. Drain the juice from the clams into the bowl. Reserve the clams. Combine 2½ cups of the clam juice with the potatoes in the saucepan and cook over medium heat, uncovered, until the potatoes are soft (about 10 minutes).
4. Add the onions and the clams to the potatoes and cook for 10 more minutes, stirring occasionally.
5. Add the evaporated milk and the butter or margarine. Turn the heat to low and cook for 15 minutes, stirring from time to time.
6. Add salt and pepper to taste. Serve in individual cups or bowls. You may want to top the chowder with oyster crackers. (Note: If you have any chowder left over, let it cool before you put it in the refrigerator. And never cool chowder with a cover on the pot. The water that condenses on the lid will turn the chowder sour.)

Maple Pumpkin Pie

Preparation and baking time: 1½ hours

Serves 8

What You Need

3 eggs
½ cup of sugar
½ cup of maple syrup
½ teaspoon of cinnamon
½ teaspoon of ginger
½ teaspoon of salt
1 16-ounce can of pumpkin
1 9-inch unbaked pie shell*
whipped cream (see "Whipping Cream," p. 8)
extra maple syrup

small mixing bowl
wire whisk or fork
measuring cup
measuring spoons
large mixing bowl
electric mixer or egg beater
medium-sized mixing bowl

What You Do

1. Preheat the oven to 400°.
2. With the wire whisk or fork, beat the eggs lightly in the small bowl.
3. Combine the beaten eggs, sugar, maple syrup, cinnamon, ginger, salt, and pumpkin in the large bowl. Beat with the mixer or egg beater until smooth.
4. Pour the mixture into the unbaked pie shell. Bake the pie on the lowest rack in the oven for 1 hour. Cool.
5. Before serving, decorate the pie with the whipped cream. Then dribble a little maple syrup on top of everything.

* You can find unbaked, frozen pie shells in the supermarket.

United States
Southeast; Midwest

My background is that of a typical midwesterner. My mother grew up on a farm in a small, rural Iowa community, and my father was a city boy from the town nearby. My parents and their parents had always lived in that area, so it was expected that I would probably settle down there, too.

Life, it seems, took a different course for me. When I was thirteen years old, we moved to Atlanta, Georgia. It was a big step for my family to take, because we had to change our life-style to fit into the southern way of living. I now wonder what it would be like if we had never left the Midwest. I can't imagine living anywhere but in the South.

Like many Americans, we have now moved again, this time to Albany, Georgia. The recipes I've chosen reflect both the Midwest and the South. The food is simple to make, but very good, I think.

Julie Thompson, 16

Oven-barbecued Brisket

Preparation and baking time: 6 hours (the meat must be refrigerated overnight)   *Serves 10–12*

What You Need

1 teaspoon of garlic salt
1 teaspoon of celery salt
1 teaspoon of onion salt
1 teaspoon of ground pepper
1 4- to 5-pound beef brisket
2 tablespoons of Liquid Smoke*
2 teaspoons of Worcestershire sauce
1 cup of bottled barbecue sauce

small mixing bowl
measuring spoons
kitchen knife
cutting board
large, shallow baking pan
aluminum foil
measuring cup

What You Do

1. In the small bowl, mix together the garlic salt, celery salt, onion salt, and pepper.
2. Trim the brisket of excess fat and place it in the baking pan.
3. Rub all sides of the brisket with the mixture of seasoning salts and pepper. Pour the Liquid Smoke over the meat. Cover the pan with foil and refrigerate overnight.
4. Preheat the oven to 300°.
5. Bake the brisket, covered with foil, for 4½ or 5 hours — until the meat is almost tender. Pour on the Worcestershire sauce and the barbecue sauce, and continue baking until the meat is tender, about half an hour longer.
6. Let the meat cool slightly so that you can cut it into thin slices. Serve the brisket hot, or later cold in sandwiches.

* This can be found, bottled, in the supermarket.

Scalloped Corn

Preparation and baking time: 1½ hours

Serves 10–12

What You Need

4 eggs
1½ cups of milk
1 teaspoon of salt
2 tablespoons of flour
2 teaspoons of sugar
1 cup of coarse cracker
    crumbs
1 20-ounce can of cream-
    style corn
butter or margarine
dash of pepper

large mixing bowl
measuring cup
measuring spoons
egg beater
long mixing spoon
2-quart casserole or 9" x 13"
    baking dish

What You Do

1. Preheat the oven to 350°.
2. Using the egg beater, mix the eggs, milk, salt, flour, and sugar together in the bowl until they are well blended.
3. Add the cracker crumbs and corn. Mix well with the mixing spoon.
4. Grease the casserole or baking dish with butter or margarine and pour in the corn mixture. Dot the top with more butter and sprinkle with pepper.
5. Bake for 1 hour, or until the mixture is firm and lightly browned.

Lemon Chess Pie

Preparation and baking time: 1 hour *Serves 8*

What You Need

2 lemons
1 stick of butter or mar-
    garine
4 eggs
2 cups of sugar
2 tablespoons of cornstarch
1 unbaked, 9-inch pie shell*
whipped cream (see "Whip-
    ping Cream," p. 8)

grater
kitchen knife
cutting board
lemon squeezer
small saucepan
medium-sized mixing bowl
fork or wire whisk
measuring cup
long mixing spoon

What You Do

1. Preheat the oven to 350°.
2. Grate the lemons (the yellow part of the rind only — not the white) and then cut them in half and squeeze them for the juice.
3. Put the stick of butter or margarine in the small saucepan and melt it over low heat.
4. Break the eggs into the bowl and beat them with the fork or wire whisk.
5. Stir in the sugar and cornstarch, then the melted butter, lemon juice, and grated rind. Mix well with the mixing spoon.
6. Pour the batter into the unbaked pie shell. Bake the pie for 45 minutes or until the filling is set and the top is lightly browned. Cool.
7. Serve each slice of pie topped with a spoonful of whipped cream.

* Unbaked, frozen pie shells are sold in supermarkets.

United States
Southwest

Our family's roots are deep in Texas, for at least four generations. You can find Gileses and Craigs all over the state, from El Paso in the west to Houston in the east.

Most people seem to think that every Texan is either a cowboy or an oil millionaire. Well, it's not true, even though Texas does have more cattle than people and pumps about one-third of all the oil in the country. We're neither, although I wouldn't mind being an oil millionaire! My dad sells houses, and my mom is a school librarian. I have an older brother in college and a sister who is in the sixth grade. I'm not sure what I want to be yet. But whatever it is, I'll do it in Texas.

I don't spend a lot of time cooking. In fact, most of the time I'd rather play soccer or tool around on my Honda. But I do like eating. And I do like making things. Here are three of my favorites. Chili I like because I can make up a big batch of it and freeze what I don't eat the first time. Three-Bean Salad is quick and goes well with almost anything. Pecan Pie doesn't need any support from me!

Craig Giles, 16

Chili with Meat
Chili con Carne

Preparation and cooking time: 3½ hours   *Serves 4*

What You Need

3 tablespoons of butter or
  olive oil
1 large onion, minced
2 cloves of garlic, minced
1 pound of ground beef
1⅓ cups of canned toma-
  toes, including the juice
1 green pepper, minced
½ teaspoon of celery seed
¼ teaspoon of cayenne
1 teaspoon of cumin seed,
  crushed*
1 small bay leaf
2 tablespoons of chili powder
⅛ teaspoon of salt
1 15-ounce can of kidney
  beans (optional)

kitchen knife
cutting board
large frying pan
measuring spoons
large saucepan
long mixing spoon

What You Do

1. Heat the butter or oil in the frying pan over medium heat. Add the onion and garlic and sauté until the onions are soft.
2. Add the meat. Mix with the onions and garlic and cook it until it is brown, stirring occasionally.
3. Transfer the meat mixture to the saucepan. Add the remaining ingredients.
4. Bring the mixture to a boil over high heat. Reduce the heat to low, and simmer, uncovered, for about 3 hours.
5. If you wish, add the kidney beans and heat through before serving.
6. Serve the chili in individual bowls with rolls or crackers.

* You can crush the cumin seed in a bowl with the back of a spoon.

Three-Bean Salad

Preparation time: ½ hour (salad must be refrigerated for an additional hour)   *Serves 10*

What You Need

1 16-ounce can of French-cut green beans
1 16-ounce can of red kidney beans
1 16-ounce can of wax beans
1 medium-sized green pepper, minced
1 medium-sized onion, minced
½ cup of salad oil
½ cup of cider vinegar
¾ cup of granulated sugar
1 teaspoon of salt
½ teaspoon of pepper

kitchen knife
cutting board
large nonmetal mixing bowl
measuring cup
medium-sized mixing bowl
wooden spoon
measuring spoons
plastic wrap

What You Do

1. Drain the beans and place them in the large bowl. Add the green pepper and onion.
2. In the smaller bowl, mix the oil and vinegar with the sugar, salt, and pepper. Pour the dressing over the bean mixture and toss.
3. Refrigerate the salad, covered with plastic wrap, for at least 1 hour before serving.

Pecan Pie

Preparation and baking time: about 1¼ hours   *Serves 8*

What You Need

2 tablespoons of butter or
  margarine
4 eggs
2 cups of dark corn syrup
1 teaspoon of vanilla
1½ cups of chopped pecans
1 unbaked 9-inch pie shell*
pecan halves for garnish
whipped cream (see "Whip-
  ping Cream," p. 8)

small saucepan
measuring cup
large mixing bowl
egg beater or wire whisk
measuring spoons

What You Do

1. Preheat the oven to 400°.
2. Melt the butter or margarine in the saucepan over low heat. Cool.
3. Break the eggs into the mixing bowl and beat them until they are smooth.
4. Beating constantly, add the corn syrup, vanilla, and cooled butter or margarine, and blend well. Stir in the pecans.
5. Pour the mixture into the pie shell. Garnish with pecan halves. Bake the pie for 35 to 40 minutes. The filling should be set at the edges but still slightly soft in the center. Cool.
6. Serve the pie with whipped cream.

* Unbaked, frozen pie shells are sold in supermarkets.

United States
Far West

I can't see how anyone would want to live anywhere but California. I know I couldn't. Our family tried it once. A few years ago we moved to Connecticut so we could be closer to the company Dad works for. He's a book salesman. It was fun, at first. Meeting new kids was cool. The change of seasons was neat, especially the fall when the leaves were so pretty. But then winter came. I didn't know there was that much ice and snow in the whole world. And hardly any sunshine. I thought the good weather would never come. I kept myself going with California Burgers and dreaming about outdoor tennis and skateboarding.

Then one day Mom and Dad said, "We're going back." Was I ever happy! Of course I miss my eastern friends. But we write to each other, and I'm sure we'll see each other again. In the meantime, I left them my two favorite California recipes. See if you don't think about California sunshine when you try them.

Jean Peddicord, 15

California Burgers

Preparation and cooking time: about ½ hour　　　　　　　　　*Serves 4*

What You Need

1 pound of ground beef
3 tablespoons of ketchup
1 teaspoon of Worcestershire
　sauce
¼ teaspoon of Tabasco
1 tablespoon of minced
　onion
1 teaspoon of prepared mus-
　tard
1 teaspoon of horseradish
¼ cup of bread crumbs
¼ teaspoon of mace
½ teaspoon of salt
4 hamburger rolls
lettuce and tomato slices
　(optional)

kitchen knife
cutting board
large mixing bowl
measuring spoons
measuring cup
long mixing spoon
broiler pan or baking pan
　with rack

What You Do

1. Put all the ingredients (except the rolls, lettuce, and tomato slices) in the bowl and mix them thoroughly.
2. Shape the mixture into 4 patties and place on the broiler pan or on the rack in the baking pan.
3. For rare burgers, broil the patties for 3 minutes on each side; for more well done burgers, broil 3–5 minutes longer.
4. Serve the burgers on toasted rolls, with lettuce and slices of tomato if desired.

Crab and Grapefruit Cocktail

Preparation time: ½ hour   *Serves 4*

What You Need

2 grapefruit
1 cup of cooked, canned
    crab meat, drained; or
    frozen King crab meat,
    thawed
3 tablespoons of orange
    juice
1 tablespoon of ketchup
¼ cup of mayonnaise

kitchen knife
grapefruit knife
cutting board
medium-sized mixing bowl
scissors
small mixing bowl
long mixing spoon
measuring spoons
measuring cup

What You Do

1. Halve the grapefruit. Remove the pulp with the grapefruit knife and cut the fruit into small pieces, discarding the seeds. Place the fruit in the larger bowl.
2. Using the scissors, snip out the membrane from the grapefruit shell.
3. Break the crab meat into bite-sized pieces, removing any membrane. Add to the grapefruit.
4. In the small bowl blend the orange juice, ketchup, and mayonnaise. Mix with the crab meat and grapefruit.
5. Fill each grapefruit shell with the mixture and serve.

Vietnam

My family and I came to the United States from Vietnam when I was fifteen. At first, we settled in Wooster, Ohio. A year later, we moved to Spokane, Washington, where I had a lot of good times. I made many friends there and learned to adjust to the American culture. Unfortunately, the program that my dad worked for was terminated in September 1977, and my family had to move once again, this time to Florida.

I love the weather here, which is almost the same as the weather in Vietnam. My three brothers, my sister, and I all attend high school. My mom and dad are community workers. We have always been a close family, and we have become even closer since we started a new life in this country.

Although I've gotten used to American food, I still prefer Vietnamese food, which we eat with chopsticks, like they do in China. Vietnamese eat a lot of rice, and Cha Gio, one of the recipes I've included here, is a dish well known to every Vietnamese. It is usually served on special occasions. I often prepare it for my parties, and most of my American friends like it. I hope you like it, too. Batter-fried Cauliflower is also a favorite Vietnamese dish, and it makes a good snack.

Tran Vu, 17

Eagle Fried Rice
Cha Gio

Preparation and cooking time: about 1 hour　　　　*Serves 4–6*

What You Need

1½ cups of white rice (not instant)
1 beef bouillon cube
1 small package of frozen green peas
1 tablespoon of oil
1 green onion, chopped
1 small onion, chopped
1 12-ounce can of Spam, Treet, or other canned ham, chopped
1 carrot, sliced
2 eggs
2 tablespoons of soy sauce
dash of pepper
dash of salt
a few sprigs of parsley, chopped

medium-sized saucepan with lid
measuring cup
vegetable peeler
kitchen knife
cutting board
small saucepan with lid
colander or sieve
large frying pan
measuring spoons
long mixing spoon

What You Do

1. In the larger saucepan cook the rice as directed on the package. While the rice is boiling, add the bouillon cube. Let the rice cool when done.
2. Cook the green peas as directed on the package. Drain them in the colander or sieve and set them aside.
3. In the frying pan, heat the oil over medium heat until it sizzles. Add the 2 kinds of onion and fry them for about 2 minutes.
4. Add the cooked rice, ham, and carrot slices to the pan and cook the mixture over medium heat, stirring occasionally, until the rice is light brown.
5. Mix in the eggs, peas, soy sauce, salt, and pepper. Simmer the mixture for about 5 minutes and serve, sprinkled with the parsley.

Batter-fried Cauliflower

```
CAUTION!
THIS RECIPE CALLS FOR FRYING IN DEEP FAT.
DO NOT GO AHEAD UNTIL YOU READ PAGE 7.
```

Preparation and cooking time: about ½ hour (batter must stand for an additional half hour)   *Serves 3*

What You Need

1½–2 cups of all-purpose
   flour
dash of salt
dash of pepper
1 12-ounce can of beer
1 medium-sized head of
   cauliflower
2 cups of cooking oil
mayonnaise

large mixing bowl
measuring cup
electric deep-fat fryer
long-handled tongs
paper towels

What You Do

1. In the large bowl, mix together the flour, salt, and pepper. Add the beer, stirring constantly to avoid lumps. (The mixture must be thick.) Let it stand for about 30 minutes.
2. Break the cauliflower into flowerets, with stems, about 1 inch thick and 2 inches long.
3. Heat the oil in the fryer until it reaches the temperature recommended by the manufacturer. Using the tongs, dip the flowerets into the batter and fry them in the hot oil until they turn light brown. Don't overcrowd the oil — cook only 5 or 6 flowerets at a time. Remove them from the oil and drain them on paper towels. Serve at once, with mayonnaise for dipping.

Cooking Terms

bake: to cook by dry heat, as in an oven

baste: to spoon liquid, fat, or a sauce over food while it is cooking

batter: an uncooked mixture, as for cakes, that can be poured; usually made of eggs, flour, and a liquid

beat: to stir or mix rapidly with a round-and-round motion, using a fork, whisk, egg beater, or electric mixer

blanch: to dip quickly into boiling water

blend: to mix two or more ingredients together until smooth

boil: to cook liquid until bubbles break the surface. A rapid boil means an active, rolling boil.

bone: to remove bones from

broil: to cook food by direct heat, either under the source of heat, as in a broiler, or over the source of heat, as on a grill

broiler-fryer: a young, meaty chicken that weighs 1½ to 4 pounds. It is an all-purpose chicken that may be roasted, simmered, or sautéed as well as broiled or fried.

broth: any clear soup, usually made with meat or fish stock

brown: to cook food at high heat until brown, usually on the stove in fat or under a broiler

casserole: a deep, heavy dish, usually with a tight-fitting lid, in which food is cooked and sometimes served. Some casseroles are only for baking in the oven; others can be used on top of the stove as well. The food cooked in a casserole is usually a combination of two or more foods.

chill: to let stand in the refrigerator until cold

chop: to cut into small pieces with a knife or chopper

clove: one of the small bulbs that make up a head of garlic; a spice

coat: to dip in another ingredient — for example, crumbs, flour, batter — before cooking

combine: to mix together so that the ingredients cannot be separated

confectioners' sugar: a finely powdered sugar

cool: to bring hot food to room temperature

cream: to work butter or margarine, often with another ingredient, until it has the consistency of whipped cream

croutons: small bread cubes sautéed or toasted in the oven

cube: to cut into cubes or squares

cutlet: a thin piece of meat for frying or broiling, usually veal or chicken

deep-fry: to cook or brown in hot liquid fat deep enough to float the food

dash: an amount smaller than ⅛ of a teaspoon

dice: to cut into fine cubes, usually ⅛″ x ¼″

dot: to distribute small bits, usually of butter, over the surface of food

dough: a pliable mixture of ingredients, usually containing flour, sugar, egg, and milk

drain: to pour off liquid

dust: to coat very lightly with flour

fillet: a boneless piece of meat or fish

flour: to coat with flour

fold: to gently add one ingredient to another without stirring or beating, by turning the ingredients in an over-and-under motion

fry: to cook or brown in hot liquid fat

frying pan: a shallow pan with a long handle, used for frying foods

garlic: a plant with a head made up of small "cloves," used for seasoning

garnish: to decorate a dish before serving; the decoration itself

giblets: the heart, liver, and gizzard of a chicken, usually in a package inside the chicken cavity

grate: to cut food into small particles by forcing it through a grater

grease: to rub with grease, such as oil, butter, or margarine

marinate: to soak food in a liquid so it will absorb the flavor of the liquid

melt: to liquefy by heating

mince: to cut into very fine pieces

mix: to stir or beat together using a round-and-round motion

mixture: a combination of two or more ingredients

panfry: to fry in just enough fat or oil to keep the food from stick-ing, or in fat or oil ¼ " to ½ " deep

pasta: a term referring to all types of macaroni—spaghetti, noo-dles, shells, and so on

peel: to remove the outer layer of skin, as from a vegetable or fruit

pickling spices: a blend of various spices—such as pepper, clove, cinnamon, and mustard—used in pickling foods

pinch: an amount that can be taken up between your thumb and forefinger. It is less than ⅛ teaspoon.

pot: a round, fairly deep cooking utensil, with or without a handle

preheat: to bring an oven or broiler to the temperature required for cooking a specific dish

Pyrex: a trademark for a type of heat-resistant glass

quarter: to cut into four equal pieces

rind: the skin or outer coat that may be peeled or taken off, as of fruit or cheese

saucepan: a somewhat deep cooking utensil, often of metal or enamel, with a handle

sauté: to cook quickly, in a little oil, butter, or margarine, over high heat, turning frequently

sear: to brown food, such as meat, briefly on the surface over high heat to seal the juices in

season: to make food more flavorful by adding salt, pepper, or other seasonings

seasoning: any added ingredient that brings out the flavor of food

set: to thicken and become firm

shred: to cut or shave food into slender pieces, as coconut

shuck: to remove the shells of clams, oysters, mussels, or scallops

sift: to pass flour or other dry ingredients through a sifter

simmer: to heat liquid just until bubbles begin to form; also, to cook food in simmering liquid over low heat

slice: to cut into thin pieces

sprinkle: to scatter small bits of a dry ingredient or drops of a liq-uid over the surface of foods

stewing chicken: a chicken between ten and twelve months old, generally weighing more than 3 pounds, with a firm flesh that needs to be tenderized by stewing *stir:* to mix with a spoon or whisk, using a round-and-round motion

stir-fry: in Chinese cooking, to fry food quickly in very little fat while stirring rapidly

stock: water in which meat or fish has been cooked

toast: to brown or make crisp and dry, usually by means of direct heat

toss: to mix lightly until well coated with a dressing, as a salad

tossed salad: a salad made from various greens and mixed with a salad dressing

vermicelli: a pasta made into slender, wormlike cords, thinner than thin spaghetti

whip: to beat until stiff, usually with a whisk, an egg beater, or an electric mixer

Equivalents

dash	=	less than ⅛ teaspoon
3 teaspoons	=	1 tablespoon
4 tablespoons	=	¼ cup
2 cups	=	1 pint
4 cups (2 pints)	=	1 quart
4 quarts	=	1 gallon
1 fluid ounce	=	2 tablespoons
8 fluid ounces	=	1 cup
16 fluid ounces	=	1 pint
32 fluid ounces	=	1 quart

Suggested Party Menus

Hors d'Oeuvres Party
Batter-fried Cauliflower (Vietnam)
Meat Turnovers (Argentina)
Danish Meatballs (Denmark)
Chicken Wings (China)
Ham Rolls (Austria)
Apple Fritters (Sicily)
Avocado Sauce and Tortilla Chips (Mexico)

Brunch
Eggs and Onions Coimbra (Portugal)
German Filled Pancakes (Germany)
Banana Cake (Puerto Rico)
Bread Pudding (Canada)

International Buffet
Oven-barbecued Brisket (United States)
Fried Rice (Polynesia)
Chicken Adobo (Philippines)
Vegetable Salad (Canada)
Irish Soda Bread (Ireland)
Trifle (Great Britain)
Shortbread Cookies (Greece)

Picnic
Fruit Soup (Israel)
Yogurt Chicken (Pakistan)
Hot Potato Salad with Bacon (Germany)
Poppy Seed Cake (Poland)
Apricot Pastries (Hungary)

Formal Dinners

1

Crab and Grapefruit Cocktail (United States)
Fried Chicken (Italy)
Stuffed Green Peppers (Albania)
Three-Bean Salad (United States)
Swedish Pancake Torte (Sweden)

2

New England Clam Chowder (United States)
Pork, Cuban Style (Cuba)
Herbed Zucchini (Italy)
Greek Salad (Greece)
Strawberries Chantilly (France)

Index